Look Away, Dixieland

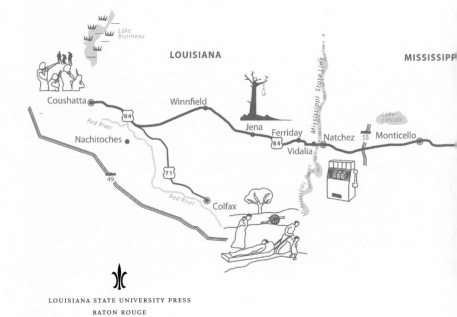

LOUISIANA

MISSISSIPPI

Lake
Bistineau

Coushatta

Red River

84

Winnfield

Jena

Ferriday

84

Vidalia

Natchez

55

Monticello

Lake
Lincoln

Mississippi State Line

Nachitoches

49

71

Red River

Colfax

LOUISIANA STATE UNIVERSITY PRESS
BATON ROUGE

LOOK AWAY
DIXIELAND

A Carpetbagger's
Great-Grandson Travels Highway 84
in Search of
the Shack-up-on-Cinder-Blocks,
Confederate-Flag-Waving, Squirrel-Hunting,
Boiled-Peanuts, Deep-Drawl,
Don't-Stop-the-Car-Here
South

James B. Twitchell

Published by Louisiana State University Press
Copyright © 2011 by James B. Twitchell
All rights reserved
Manufactured in the United States of America
First printing

Designer: Michelle A. Neustrom
Typeface: Whitman
Printer: McNaughton & Gunn, Inc.
Binder: Dekker Bookbinding

Map of road trip on the title page is by Susan Duser.

Library of Congress Cataloging-in-Publication Data

Twitchell, James B., 1943–
    Look away, Dixieland : a carpetbagger's great-grandson travels Highway 84
in search of the shack-up-on-cinder-blocks, Confederate-flag-waving, squirrel-
hunting, boiled-peanuts, deep-drawl, don't-stop-the-car-here South / James B.
Twitchell.
        p. cm.
    ISBN 978-0-8071-3761-1 (cloth : alk. paper)
1. Twitchell, James B., 1943– —Travel—Southern States—Anecdotes.
2. Twitchell, James B., 1943– —Family—Anecdotes. 3. Southern States—
Description and travel—Anecdotes. 4. Southern States—Social life and
customs—Anecdotes. 5. Southern States—History—Anecdotes. I. Title.
    F216.2.T84 2011
    975—dc22
                                                                    2010038062

To MHT

Contents

Illustrations

Look Away, Dixieland

Introduction
Deep in the Heart of Dixie

There is no truth but in transit.
—RALPH WALDO EMERSON

I have two stories to tell. One is about a trip I took across the Deep South, and the other is about my great-grandfather, who, for a while, lived there. I think of these stories as the vertical and horizontal axes of my sense of Dixieland. The vertical one is my family history going back to when "Dixie" really caught the American imagination, namely, after the Civil War. And the horizontal axis is my literal trip in 2009 across a narrow ribbon of the midsections of Georgia, Alabama, Mississippi, and Louisiana. My hope is that, as with the X and Y axes of dreaded algebra, plotting a point in one story may somehow sooner or later connect me to a point in the other. In other words, historical events don't go away; the past lingers in the present. And geographical places don't exist merely on the surface; they are rooted in culture. So here's one of the questions of this book: Can you travel across the present and somehow connect to a past event? Or, to borrow an image from science fiction, can you, like Marty McFly in *Back to the Future*, hop into the DeLorean time machine and drive back along present-day two-lane blacktop into Reconstruction Dixie?

My great-grandfather was a carpetbagger. He lived in Coushatta, Louisiana, after the Civil War. A big chunk of his family moved there too. A lot of them got killed. He got his arms shot off. Coushatta is on the banks of the Red River, just below Shreveport. I live in northern Florida, on the east side of Dixieland. Here's the crux of this book: If I drive slowly across the region, will I come to understand better what happened to my kin in the 1870s? Can I find a path across the South that will duplicate enough of the world my great-grandfather and his family experienced so that I can have an understanding of what happened to them? And, if so, will Spinoza be right: is to understand all to forgive all? Or, to be more realistic, is to be able to understand a little bit to be able to forgive a little bit?

Here are some of the things I want to understand by intersecting the stories of family history with a literal journey across the South: How much of my sense of the Deep South is created by stories told in the faraway North and in the Hollywood west? What are the limits of southern culture in absorbing the foreign, the Other, the Yankee? How come the South is so violent (or is that just part of media-made Dixie)? Why is Dixieland still proud of behavior it knows is rebellious (or is that just contrived bravado)? What is the role of honor and blood, and does this still motivate behavior, especially of white males? How important is topography (swampy) and climate (moist) to culture? How come the South is known for down-home hospitality when there seems to be such a history of you-keep-out? Is the South really all about race? How could Reconstruction have been so right and yet have been done so wrong? Why is the Southern Baptist religion so popular? Why didn't blacks burn the place down in the 1960s? What is the obsession with landowning and bloodlines? How come they have such great writers and musicians? How come McCain did better than George W in only one place in the country, namely, in a narrow swath across Deep Dixie; and, well, you get the point. Like a pesky little brat pulling at his mother's skirts, I want to know about the South.

First, let me map out the horizontal path of my trip—the X axis. And then, in the first chapter, I'll try to explain the more complicated vertical path of family stories—the Y axis. Let's assume that there really is such a place as the Deep South that still exists today. As opposed to most other sections of the country (eastern seaboard, New England, Rust Belt, Southwest, Pacific Northwest, and the like), Dixieland is markedly different from the rest of the United States. And, unlike most of the other sections, this difference has been preserved over time. You can hear it in the accents and stories, you can taste it in the food, you can see it in their eyes, you can read about it in their novels, you can smell it in magnolia and pulp mills, and you can be lectured about it by Yankees who claim it's about to disappear. That it doesn't change much is part of what makes it Dixie.

Here's what I mean. For a brief shining moment back in the late 1990s, some commentators thought that this South was about to transform (*Dixie Rising: How the South Is Shaping American Values, Politics, and Culture*, by the *New York Times* Atlanta bureau chief Peter Applebome, and V. S. Naipaul's occasionally brilliant articles for the *New Yorker* reprinted as *A Turn in the South*). But not much happened. In truth, taps had been played for Dixie before: Harry Ashmore's *An Epitaph for Dixie* back in the 1950s and even before that by the New South movement in the 1870s. As W. J. Cash observed in the early 1940s in his wonderfully loopy *The Mind of the South*, we Americans, especially Yankees, like to think of the South as changing: the idea of the Reborn South, the Rising South, the Advancing South is part of how the South exists in communal imaginations (179–82). Has any product from Procter & Gamble had *new* stuck in front of it more than the South? Yet, for all the announcements of incipient change, much of the Deep South seems preserved in amber and pine pitch.

When the Heart of Dixie reverts to type, as it did in the presidential election of 2008, no one writes anguished books about it like *What's the Matter with Kansas?* because, at some level, it's almost expected. There is no book called "What's the Matter with Alabama/Mississippi/Louisiana?" because we all think we know what's the matter with Dixie. As if to taunt the pundits, Dixie's not just slow to change, it seems to have little interest in change.

And so the region is still regularly ridiculed in movies, television, books, and Web sites. Only music ever defends it, and even then often with a good ol' boy wink. It's not coincidental that country music is the only national entertainment actually produced in the South—Nashville. Pop music sings a different song, however. Listen to Billy Joel's anthem "We Can't Stop the Fire," a veritable catalog of American life as seen from New York a generation ago, and you'll hear not one complimentary reference to the South. Instead the allusions are to Selma, Orval Faubus,

Ole Miss, and, of course, Dallas. The South is the only part of the country that has become so entrenched in our bicoastal imaginations that merely its mention makes the rest of us jumpy. Just mention *Deliverance, Easy Rider,* and *Cape Fear* to an aging Yuppie and you'll see what I mean. That anxiety can even be seen under the protective guise of parody: think *The Dukes of Hazzard, Hee Haw,* Sheriff Buford T. Justice of the *Smokey and the Bandit* movies, Zed in *Pulp Fiction,* and even Jeff Foxworthy's redneck routines ("you know you're a redneck if . . .). Forget about the real stuff, like Dixie itself, our Dixiephobia seems stuck in place.

Remember now, I'm really talking Heart of Dixie, the cracker South, the white-trash South, the boll-weevil, moon-pie, fire-ant, palmetto, sweet-ice-tea, kudzu, chicken-fried-steak, and armadillo South. I'm talking about the South still left over from the Civil War. This is *not* the Peachtree Plaza/Atlanta South, the big-banks-going-bankrupt-in-Charlotte South, the I-4 Corridor in Orlando South, the Research Triangle South, or the why-don't-they-fix-it-New Orleans South. Nor is it the Montgomery, Mobile, Memphis, Nashville, Wilmington, Jackson, Natchez South. I'm after backcountry South, down South, Deep South, real South. Few people are reading *Southern Living* on the porch swing and drinking merlot in the South I want to traverse and understand. This is the shack-up-on-cinder-blocks South, Confederate-flag-waving South, squirrel-hunting South, Jeeter Lester and Flem Snopes South, vultures-having-possum-lunch-in-the-road South, boiled-peanuts, deep-drawl South, for-God's-sake-don't-stop-the-car-here South.

To understand this area, as it is now and as it might have been when my great-grandfather lived in it, I want to put down the book and put the rubber to the road. I admit it's a drive-by understanding that I'm after, but I think it might be more rewarding than a read-about or a watch-a-movie understanding. After all, I've lived in this South for the last thirty years, and I really don't understand a lot of it. So I want to mosey across the culture that literally lies between Interstate 20 in the north (that goes Atlanta–Birmingham–Jackson) and Interstate 10 along the Gulf Coast (that goes Pensacola–Mobile–New Orleans). When you look at a map, you'll see the obvious route: it's U.S. Highway 84, a floppy snake of a road running from mid-Georgia through lower Alabama and Mississippi, turning a few degrees north in Louisiana to cross the upper half of

Texas, then cutting the corner of New Mexico to collapse at the base of
the Rocky Mountains in southern Colorado. This is not the Dixie-rising
South; this is the Fallen-and-I-can't-get-up Dixie South. This is the X axis
of my southern algebra, the horizontal east-to-west path that hopefully
will touch the Y points of my family history. Here's what it looks like:

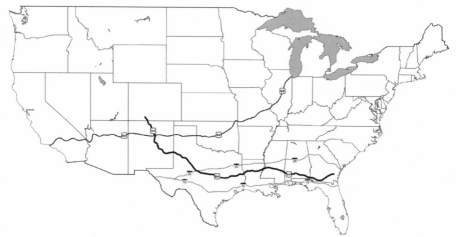

The entirety of U.S. Highway 84 from I-95 in Georgia to Pagosa Springs, Colorado.
This highway runs between I-20 and I-10 and may well become I-14.
Map by Susan Duser

The Rig

I knew that to properly understand the culture of U.S. 84 I was going
to have to slow everything down. I didn't want to do it in a car, I'm too
old to walk, too wobbly to bike, and the DeLorean DMC-12 plutonium-
fueled time machine is taken. What I really needed was a slow-moving
sofa. Now, when a middle-aged man heads out on a road trip like this,
like it or not, the first thing you hear about is his transportation, his
wheels, his sofa. So when John Steinbeck heads out in *Travels with Charley,* we get introduced to the conversion pickup truck he names Rocinante, after Don Quixote's horse. When William Least Heat-Moon pulls
on to the blue highways, he wants you to know about his Econoline
van with the bunk in the back that he calls Ghost Dancing. Bill Bryson
(*The Lost Continent: Travels in Small-Town America*) rather sheepishly

5

admits he's driving his mom's rusted Chevy Chevette, called Chevette. Larry McMurtry (*Roads: Driving America's Great Highways*) gossips along various interstates in the front seat of full-sized sedans from the rental companies he names; Charles Kuralt pontificates from the pulpit of CBS television's land yachts, GMC motor homes, to be specific; James Morgan (*The Distance to the Moon: A Road Trip into the American Dream*) is on the take from Porsche and so sings paeans to the new Boxter; Robert Pirsig (*Zen and the Art of Motorcycle Maintenance*) philosophizes from his 1964 Honda SuperHawk bike seat, and so it goes. No sooner does the key go into the ignition than the romancing of the rig starts.

So here's what I drove slow-motion across Dixie—a relatively sedate motor home, also called a recreational vehicle, an RV. It came with a name: the Winnebago View. In the company of Steinbeck, Least Heat-Moon, and Bryson, how mortifying to be driving something called a View. What the hell's a View?

The middle-aged sojourner, realizing that he needs to name his steed —and that the best names, Rocinante and Ghost Dancing, have already been taken—lets the PR flacks for the RV company do it for him. They usually follow what I call the developer-destroying mandate, which dictates that a developer calls his mall (or housing development) by the name of the very thing he destroyed when construction began. So Meadowbrook, Rosedale, Briarwood, Woodlawn, Crabtree Valley, Twelve Pines all point to what used to be there before the earthmover arrived.

In such a spirit, the RV-namers help their paunchy consumers with names like Arctic Fox, Bambi, Mountain Aire, Wildcat—all the stuff your RV destroys. In this context, View makes some sense. This bubble of pig iron and plastic sits right in the middle of somebody else's view. The name could be worse. Sometimes the aspiration mandate takes hold and accounts for such names as the Banshee, Prowler, Wanderer, Weekend Warrior, and, my favorites, the Bounder and the Intruder. En route to studying the Deep South, my wife and I used to wander through RV parks noting the names of motor homes and quietly smirking, conveniently forgetting that we were filling up space with our . . . View. Alas, we never could find a proper name for it. View is so Vanilla. For a while we tried Mother Ship, then Prius, and finally we just settled for Thing.

Now of course as an academic I'm trained to think these motor homes are just awful, the wheeled coffins that midwesterners drive to Florida to die in. They are road and gas hogs, bellying up to the road trough, taking up our space, yet one more chapter in the Tragedy of the Commons. However, if you are going to take a slowpoke, look-see trip across this country, these are the wheels to use. "A View with a Room," as the *New York Times* cutely called it in a generally forgiving review (May 24, 2009). You can move fifty miles a day, walk the dog, sit around and read, chat up the locals, or take a nap. What you don't have to do is speed down the interstate and then hole up in the Holiday Inn. You can meander down the road and then hole up in somebody's backyard or in the Walmart parking lot.

Why This Route?

Here's another of my endless questions: How deep is the Deep South? To what extent does it really exist, and to what extent is it a territory of the hegemonic imagination, as my colleagues might say, just another cultural construct like race, class, gender, and . . . geography? I've often thought it portentous that the two anthems of southern regionalism—"Way Down upon the Swanee River" and "Dixie"—were both written by Yankees who rarely, if ever, set foot south of the Mason-Dixon line. Such an irony that even the southern view of the South is partially imported from the North.

So, for instance, I wanted to find out what literally lies along this road, the stuff tossed overboard, the garbage. Is it southern trash or northern trash? For a while I even thought I'd stop each day at some appointed hour and collect litter from the roadside and examine it for clues. But, as you'll see, I only did this as far as Alabama. There was simply too much of it.

If you ever read travel books, you know the general rule is, as Paul Theroux observed, that the trashier the road, the better the trip. From the look of Highway 84, we're in for a good time: it's a bit of a mess. If this road doesn't take you through the middens of Dixie, no road does. U.S. 84 has to be about the most depressing east-west passage in the country—Route 66's evil twin. U.S. 66 goes from bustling Chicago to laid-back Santa Monica. Heaven. U.S. 84 goes from low swamp to high desert. Hell. If U.S. 66 is the "Mother Road," as Steinbeck called it in *The Grapes of Wrath*, then U.S. 84 is the forgotten cousin off at reform school. On its eastern end, it doesn't even make the Atlantic. The eastern terminus is an Interstate 95 off ramp near the Okefenokee Swamp. In the west, it burrows into a sandbank around Pagosa Springs, Colorado.

But interesting for travelers at the beginning of the twenty-first century is that if you were to set a map of U.S. 84 over a political cartogram (in which the sizes of states were rescaled for population, not acreage), you would see that this highway almost exactly bisects the narrow band of 2008 McCain voters. Compare this with how Bush did four years earlier, and you will see that here McCain polled far better. This roadway is not necessarily a Republican stronghold. Quite the contrary, not long ago Republicans were despised. Clearly, something else is going on. Turn these data inside out and you'll see. More than political concerns, it seems knee-jerk reactive. If you ever wanted to find the wellspring of the current distrust of Obama, you couldn't do better than to follow this path. In a sense, U.S. 84 is the Rush Limbaugh/Glenn Beck National Highway. Along its route many people don't just watch Fox News, they believe Fox News. The white culture is not pro-McCain as much as it's anti–African American. And I think it's not anxious about Obama as a man or Obama as a politician as much as it's profoundly shocked about Obama as a black man in power.

I don't make the observation above out of regional snobbery. It's just that I don't share this particular anxiety. As a kid, I was hand-fed different stories. I grew up forty miles south of the Quebec border. I believed that the French Canadians, the Québécois, were shiftless workers, lousy drivers, and eager to intermarry with Protestants in order to repair their obvious genetic deficiencies. I remember my grandmother pulling me aside and whispering that if JFK became president, the pope would soon be calling the shots. I was afraid the Québécois would rise up. About this time in the 1950s, a black man did come to Vermont. He was a minister. I remember seeing pictures of him in the newspaper. My fellow Vermonters, great-grandsons of righteous abolitionists, filled his front door with buckshot and threw small dead animals up onto his porch. Driving

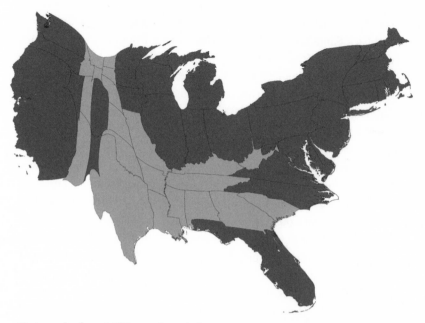

Cartograph of 2008 U.S. presidential election. Highway 84, if laid over this map, would almost exactly bisect the gray area—the band of McCain voters.

Courtesy Mark Newman, Department of Physics and Center for the Study of Complex Systems, University of Michigan, www-personal.umich.edu/~mejn/election/2008/

west on U.S. 84, I couldn't help but wonder what prejudice-rich stories would now be filling my head had I grown up here in Dixie.

So don't confuse this Deep South 84 with all the other forgettable 84s. This one is unique and special. Stories here are different. Like Vegas, what happens here stays here. And it stays for generations. California has a state highway 84 in the Bay Area. Meanwhile, two interstate 84s lie on either side of the country, one going Oregon to Utah and the other from mid-Pennsylvania to the Mass Pike. When I told my long-suffering wife we were going to be inching along Highway 84, she was pleased. We sometimes drive part of the latter across the slowly rolling hills en route to Vermont. Then I showed her my 84. This one, I assured her, was the *real deal* 84.

I could see that she was not good for the whole route, and so I hedged a bit by saying that I was not going all the way, only from Waycross,

Georgia, to just below Shreveport, Louisiana—the southern crescent. Why those two spots? Because Waycross is due north of me, and just below Shreveport is the little town of Coushatta, where my great-grandfather settled his family after the Civil War. It's right on 84. It's right at the edge of where the South ends and the West begins. If only things had turned out differently, that part of Louisiana might now be my home. Lots of people got killed there, many, many more than my family members. Most of them were black. In fact, U.S. 84 traverses one of the most notorious killing fields in American history, right on the banks of the Red River. Few people have paid attention to these slaughters. I'm going to focus on them. I hope learning about the culture along U.S. 84 as I move west from Georgia will prepare me for what I know is out there in Louisiana.

In terms of my algebraic taxonomy, these killing fields are ground zero of the Y axis. I think they go straight into the heart of the Deep South. In fact, I think that one could make a case that it was the slow, bloody wrenching of the 1870s and not the relatively fast, bloody battles of the 1860s that gave the South its sense of Dixie. It was then, after the war and well into the twentieth century, that the Confederate battle flag started to take on its iconic meaning. And those battles are still being fought.

The Road Ahead: A Path-ology

One nice thing about U.S. 84 is that no notable American road-tripper— Jack Kerouac, John Steinbeck, William Least Heat-Moon, Vladimir Nabokov, Bill Bryson, V. S. Naipaul—has ever spent much time on it. They cross it going elsewhere. Had it been in place, Alexis de Tocqueville would have delicately taken his French leave. The only explorer I imagined who might have been willing to spend any time on this road would have been the indomitable William Bartram (*Travels through North and South Carolina, Georgia, East and West Florida*, 1791), who seems happy in the most godforsaken places. U.S. 84 is terra incognita.

Even the locals who live along it seem confused with what to do with this road. A few years ago, the southern states bisected by U.S. 84 petitioned the federal government to at least give the highway a better name. In 1989, they did. In gov-speak, the Feds christened the highway the El Camino East/West Corridor, but only from mid-Texas to Interstate 95 in Georgia. The government put up little signs along the road to this effect. But the locals knew better. Although supposedly based on a Spanish "royal road" (*el camino real*) connecting its New World colonies of Mexico and Florida, this road had absolutely nothing to do with ancient migration or trade patterns between Mexico and the southern United States. The highfalutin name was a complete charade, a NAFTA-inspired attempt to increase trade and a bit of Babbitry by tourist bureaus to create faux history.

In truth, U.S. 84 was not a west-to-east route of imaginary Spanish conquistadores looking for some Eldorado or a way to connect the dots of the Spanish empire; it was a secondary east-to-west route for Scots/Irish overflow from Virginia, Georgia, and the Carolinas looking for fresh topsoil. Before the Civil War, after these Celts overfarmed their fragile land with cotton and sometimes sugar and tobacco, they inched west following old Indian trails. Often they took a slave or two with them, but most of these settlers were simple yeomen who could barely care for themselves. That's the unheroic and decidedly unromantic history of U.S. 84.

The road might better be called Overflow Alley or Tuckered-out Turnpike because the movement along it was not to find the New World but to leave the old. It was not western aspirational (Chisholm Trail, Santa Fe Trail, Oregon Trail . . .) but eastern exhausted. It was used to get away from, not to get to. Once you get on U.S. 84 you can see why it's more usually called the Wiregrass Highway—that spike weed is all over the place. Tourist bureaus of individual states have coined tourist-friendly names. Georgia, for instance, names U.S. 84 as one of the state's five scenic routes, Pines & Plantations, but the name won't stick.

Now all this having been said, in one of the ironies of marketing, the great modern migration that has been occurring along U.S. Highway 84 is indeed from the Spanish-speaking South, not the legacy of a royal road of the conquistadores but the reality of a well-beaten path of migrant workers. Their movement is now west to east. All along this El Camino East/West Corridor, Mexican laborers have been inching up from south Texas to take jobs the locals passed by, most famously in meatpacking plants. One of the largest busts of undocumented workers occurred in August 2008 in Laurel, Mississippi, about halfway across El Camino, when almost 350 mostly Mexicans were arrested at a transformer factory. You don't need news reports to point out this migration pattern, however. Just look out the car window to see who's doing most of the stooped-over field labor.

U.S. 84 may now be at a crossroads. Around the turn of the twenty-first century, the Feds forecast that a new interstate, so-called Interstate 14, would be built over U.S. 84—literally piggybacked over the existing road. The real promise of Interstate 14, née U.S. 84, was that it would make their cloverleaf culture look just like every other cloverleaf culture in the United States. Tourism would flourish. Mississippi even started four-laning its section and erecting the blue-background exit signs to announce the burger, gas, and motel franchises. Thank goodness, although a few high-rise signs are up, Interstate 14 is not. The recession got there first. Appropriations were cut. So I especially wanted to get on this highway before the appropriations were restored and this passage became just another section of predictable asphalt, gas pumps, and french fries. As Charles Kuralt, another sojourner of the back road, has observed, the interstate highway system makes it possible to travel from coast to coast without seeing anything.

The Guidebooks

Along with famous road-trippers, guidebooks routinely neglect U.S. 84. Don't look for it in Fodor's *The South* or even *Southern Living's Travel South*. Not a peep. Ditto: *Road Trip USA: Cross-Country Adventures on America's Two-Lane Highways*. The Lonely Planet series has a guidebook called *Deep South: Louisiana, Mississippi, Alabama*. With the exception of a few paragraphs about wiregrass and pine trees in Alabama, U.S. 84 is completely passed by. Lonely Planet is written for foreigners. Rand Mc-Nally has a *Getaway Guide to the Southeast*, filled with maps and commentary. It's written for Americans. They have a special section called "Best of the Road Trips: A Drive through the Deep South." Not a mention.

The only books that have taken this road (and are quite taken by it) are the guides done by the Federal Writers' Project of FDR's Works Progress Administration (WPA) near the end of the Great Depression. These were the glory days of U.S. 84. and in each of the massive tomes (running to more than five hundred pages dedicated to an individual state), a handful of uncredited writers (to credit just a few: Conrad Aiken, Nelson Algren, Saul Bellow, John Cheever, Malcolm Cowley, Edward Dahlberg, Ralph Ellison, Zora Neale Hurston, Kenneth Patchen, Philip Rahv, Kenneth Rexroth, Harold Rosenberg, Studs Terkel, Richard Wright) lovingly trace the route, mile by mile.

These guides are fun to read even if your only trip is to the refrigerator. John Steinbeck rhapsodizes about them in *Travels with Charley: In Search of America:*

> [The guides were] compiled during the Depression by the best writers in America, who were, if that is possible, more depressed than any other group while maintaining their inalienable instinct for eating. But the books were detested by Mr. Roosevelt's opposition. If WPA workers leaned on their shovels, the writers leaned on their pens. The result was that in some states the plates were broken up after a few copies were printed, and that is a shame because they were reservoirs of organized, documented and well-written information, geological, historic and economic. (1962 Viking edition, 134)

Steinbeck is not alone appreciating them. When John Gunther hit the road for his memoir *Inside U.S.A.* (1947), his trunk was full of the WPA guides, and William Least Heat-Moon clearly has them open on the seat while driving through the Midwest writing *PrairyErth (a deep map)* (1991).

Happily, all the WPA guidebooks for my trip along U.S. 84—Georgia, Alabama, Mississippi, Louisiana—are in good order and easy to obtain. Before I took off, I devoured them all, cover to cover. These guides were to be my shoestring Baedekers. Although their racial politics were notoriously bad (as we will see), the guides were insightful about the entrenched culture. The writers understood that Deep Dixie was obsessed not with *lost* but with *loss,* not with *guilt* but with *shame,* not with *war* but with *Reconstruction.* "Ferget hell, Fergive never" is not about Appomattox, but about the agony that followed. These writers understood that the Deep South is many things, not the least an emotional state. It lives roiled up, unable or unwilling to get on with it, to get past it. Dixie circa 1938 was much like Dixie circa 1883. Postbellum malaise is not a touted theme of the books, but between the lines you do get a sense of separation, of depression, of isolationism, even of hopelessness. In a sense, the real Civil War in this South was fought in the 1870s and 1880s. On the surface, at least, Dixie won this war. Or so it thought. The guides know better.

So in a sense, even before setting foot on it, one can see that this is a road that can be understood as a path across the state of Melancholy, in which survival itself is a test for success. Not being crushed is a goal. Right below the red neck, there's a chip on its shoulder, a whiff of Wanna make something of it? to this section of the country. To be crossing the Deep South at the same time that the worldwide financial markets were tanking seemed weirdly propitious. Every time I turned on the radio, I heard that things around the country were indeed *going south*. Well, so were we. Occasionally we felt that this section of the country and the entire culture were finally in some strange kind of synch.

The Unreliable Narrator

It may sound a little highfalutin to consider this road across this part of the country as a passage through a state of suspended consciousness, a kind of freeze-frame, flip card of a world after Reconstruction and before modernity, the X axis of Dixie, but that's my working assumption. I'm fully aware that I, a seventh-generation Vermonter who currently lives in north Florida (culturally, south Georgia) and teaches school, may not be a trustworthy chronicler of what lies along this path. I'm not even sure of the genre of the work you're holding in your hands. Is there such a thing as a historical-quest-travelogue? A geriatric picaresque?

William Faulkner famously said he had to make up Yoknapatawpha County, a postage stamp of fictional Southland, because the real stuff was simply too complex for him to handle. "To understand the world, you must first understand a place like Mississippi," he said, not entirely talking about Mississippi. What he says is true not just about the South, but really about the impossibility of understanding any place, maybe Dixieland only more so. But, as cultural anthropologists like to retort, with obvious self-interest, the least responsible reporters of life in the aquarium are the fish.

All these caveats aside, I may still be less dependable than many fellow fish. First, although I live in the Deep South, I spend most of my time trying to stay out of it. Gainesville, Florida, the home of the University of Florida, is a little island of anxious guppies in a sea of redneck gators. I've lived here for more than thirty years, yes, but I live in a fortified aquarium. After every election you can see my Alachua County, a little splotch of blue against a sea of red.

Ironically, these Deep Southerners probably understand me better than I understand them. After all, the national media are delivered in my language, and even regional stations (with the exception of the farm reports) broadcast drawl-free. In really rural places, I often can't understand a single word I hear. How in the hell am I going to understand what someone says in Waynesboro, Mississippi, when I don't even know what "finer than frog hair" or "meat and three sides" means, let alone the difference between dip, snuff, and chew?

Years ago we bought a little place in the country, what in the North would be called a *camp*, but down here is called a *lake place*. Along with the building I inherited a yard man who had long worked there for the previous owner. In my mind, he came with the place. I was mortified. It was like I was a slaveholder. But that wasn't the problem. My wife had to translate our conversations. And it was not because he was black. There is a roadhouse not far from the lake place called Chappini's. Since they've been serving beer since the 1930s, they have been grandfathered past the restriction that you must drink inside. The clientele is almost all white. You can stand outside in the afternoon and drink beer watching the pickup trucks go by. I like going there. But I often can't understand a word that's said. I'm usually feeling: Hurry up! Make your point! Speak English, dammit! Bill Bryson, midwesterner-turned-New Englander, says what I've felt, "The average Southerner has the speech patterns of someone slipping in and out of consciousness" (*The Lost Continent*, 2001, 69).

But it works both ways. They probably think I sound like an endless old Edison tinfoil cylinder. Listening to me, I'm sure they're thinking of the great line from *Cool Hand Luke* when Strother Martin whines through his nose, "What we've got here is a failure to communicate." In the Deep South, let's face it, I'm the stranger in a strange land. However, now that I'm in my mid-sixties, it's time that I pay attention to this world around me and try to at least understand its strangeness. I've kept it at arm's length long enough. Time to heave-to, hit the road, go off to confront my ancient kinsmen. Plus, I have a confession to make. Although I don't always understand Dixie, I like it a lot. Often I tire of smug Yankees telling me not just what to do but how to feel about it. I admit it—a lot of me is redneck.

I think that my transplanted status would have been okay with my great-grandfather. I think he intended for me to be a southerner, albeit a well-behaved one. To explain this, however, I have to now jump to the endpoint of my trip, those killing fields in upstate Louisiana—the Y axis, as it were. For understanding what happened over there is the primary goal of my trip. What happened on the banks of the appropriately named Red River in midstate Louisiana could have happened only in one place in the United States—the Deep South. No other section of the country spills blood like this. So, ironically, maybe that's where this road trip starts, over at the end, in Coushatta, Louisiana, about 140 years ago. I hope it's not portentous, but the first gear of this road trip is to jam things into neutral. Before we climb up on the sofa and hit the road, I've got to get out and plot some points on the other axis of this Dixieland graph.

①

My Great-Grandfather

Mistah Kurtz—he dead.

A penny for the Old Guy

—T. S. ELIOT, "THE HOLLOW MEN"

To understand the Deep South, you must first understand Reconstruction, and to understand Reconstruction, you need to understand the morality play that is late nineteenth-century American history, and to understand this morality play, you need to know the stock characters, the dramatis personae, as it were. The drama of Reconstruction features vice characters who play out prescribed roles, thereby giving coherence to what was in truth a simply terrible mess. To make sure the play works in cleaning up the mess, there can be little variation in the behavior of these stereotypes.

So here they are stage center: the white-haired colonel, the dispossessed veteran, the crinolined demoiselle, the confused darkie, the wounded hero, the duplicitous scalawag, the tender-hearted Mammy, and, over there in the dark corner twisting his waxed mustache, the villain of the piece—the carpetbagger. Before leaving the stage and heading back up north, he's furiously stuffing dollar bills and silver candlesticks into his satchel, foreclosing on the widow's property and stealing the votes of the newly enfranchised African Americans. Here's what he looks like:

Carpetbagger cartoon by Thomas Nast, *Harper's Weekly*, November 9, 1872
The Granger Collection, New York

The Cunning Fox Which Joins the Coon, plate 11 of *Comus Parade during Mardi Gras*, 1873
Historic New Orleans Collection

How these carpetbaggers were escorted to the door is, I think, one of the most important acts in the play. In fact, I think it's the climax, the cresting action, the defining moment of Dixie. It's the Y axis. Often in our bowdlerized version we simply skip act 5, scene 4, preferring to bring the curtain down and get to more pleasant stories. Somehow the damn Yankees exit stage left. But here's what historians are finding: the expulsion of carpetbaggers was anything but neat. Sometimes it was really bloody. They got the hook literally, so to speak. And what made it traumatic for the South was that it could not be bundled up in race. This was white attacking white, and it was often done in massacres by local death squads. And it happened all across the South, all along the X axis, in almost every town currently bisected by U.S. 84.

So since this vice character is crucial in setting the play into action and since his expulsion was so defining of the complexities of southern culture, I'd like to introduce you to my great-grandfather. This information may put some ambiguity into the stereotype, making him a bit more human, and perhaps making the morality play less efficient in passing on cherished interpretations. No matter: here's what I knew about my carpetbagger and when I knew it.

When I was about twelve years old, my father got a letter from some graduate student in Louisiana who was writing a master's thesis on my dad's granddad, Marshall Harvey Twitchell. By any chance, did we have his papers? This letter seemed to come out of the blue, but it caused quite a commotion among us up in northern Vermont. I had no idea that my dad had inherited a literal carpetbag full of memorabilia, a trove of mysterious photos, newspaper clippings, letters, two wonderful swords (one tarnished with the names of battles inscribed on the scabbard and the other silvery sleek in a shiny black scabbard, both of which I spent considerable time brandishing à la D'Artagnan), as well as a massive moldy scrapbook.

My great-grandfather had even written an autobiography. The copy we had was an onion-skin carbon in blue ink. It almost cracked apart in your hands. I couldn't have cared less. For the most part it was old stuff that fell apart when you touched it so I was supposed to keep my hands off. My dad said someday I would be interested and to quit playing with the swords before someone got hurt. I remember him also saying that everyone reaches an age when family history becomes important and that my time would come. I also remember seeing pictures of my parents presenting a bundle of this stuff to a university library in Louisiana.

Judging by how my family reacted to this request for information and the fact that this stuff was ending up in a library, it was clear that this Marshall Harvey Twitchell was a big deal. He was somebody special. The reason was obvious, at least to me. In pictures he had no arms—just plastic hands at the end of his sleeves.

Here's a bit of who he was. He was a carpetbagger who sought fame and fortune in the Deep South after the Civil War. But it's not so simple as the morality play of high school history played it out. Maybe just the opposite. As I heard the story, he grew up on rocky farmland in central Vermont. In the 1850s, he was caught up in war fever. He enlisted as a private in the Fourth Vermont Brigade. He got more than he bargained for, saw a lot of action, and was twice left for dead. But when the war was over, he didn't come home. At least not right away.

After being passed over for promotion, my great-grandfather took a position as a captain of company H of the Texas 109th Regiment USCT (United States Colored Troops) and went off to fight skirmishes in Texas. By all accounts, including his own, he got along well with black people and was happy in the United States Colored Troops. Still not allowed to muster out because of his recent reenlistment, he looked for alternate work inside the army. He took a job as a provost marshal and agent of the Freedmen's Bureau for the parish of Bienville, Louisiana.

He was now entering the role that would make him famous/infamous. As an administrator of the so-called Reconstruction in the South, he was sent by the Feds to northwestern Louisiana, just south of Shreveport near the Red River. Here he was sheriff, judge, town planner, tax collector, problem resolver, school board organizer, and the voice of faraway control from Washington, D.C. Most important, he oversaw labor contracts between ex-slaves and employers. He was a capable administrator and did well in the demanding job of merging interests of exuberant blacks, cocky Unionists, and deflated Confederates. For a while.

For a man who had spent the previous decade almost continually on the march, my great-grandfather was clearly settling down. And I mean

Marshall Harvey Twitchell as American consul in Kingston, Ontario. Note the fake arms and hands.

Photo from author's collection

settling, because within a year he courted and married the daughter of an ex-Confederate cotton planter. Perhaps this did not endear him to the local protectors of the Lost Cause, but it did give him a sense of an in-place southern family. And it certainly fit the stereotype of the plundering Yankee, now robbing the South even of its belles.

In truth, his bride, Adele Coleman, seems to have been complicit. She clearly had set her cap for this young man who was off on his own, far from home. If you look at her letters and his autobiography, you will see that, at twenty, she found rebellion more than a little romantic. In spite of her parents' protestations and her brother's active opposition, she had run into the arms of this intruding Yankee. She even insisted that he wear his Union uniform at their wedding. At some level, they were stereotypes in the drama of Reconstruction: carpetbagger and southern belle.

Here the morality play takes some turns. MHT (as I shall call him from here on because I have trouble calling him by his name/my name) did well, and in doing well, he allowed his in-laws to prosper. Finally mustered out of service in 1866, he could have gone back to Vermont with his bride. But Adele was becoming sickly with what was to become tuberculosis, and it was clear that he liked the South. As well, maybe he saw a chance to make a fortune. Or maybe he could remember what life was like in rocky Vermont. Did he really want to take her there? Did he himself really want to go back? Why farm rocks when you can drain a bayou and find some of the richest soil in the world? Why freeze half the year when you can bask in the sunshine? He clearly liked the South.

His southern roots grew deeper each month. He was sinking the Y axis of my tale. With his in-laws, he purchased adjoining plantations on Lake Bistineau in Bienville Parish. Then he bought a plantation to the south on the Red River called Starlight Plantation. In 1870 he was elected to the state senate. Whites supported him. To operate his new properties, MHT brought his brother, Homer, and brother-in-law George King down from the North; then down came Homer's wife, his mother, another sister, Helen, and her husband, M. C. Willis, and finally his sister Kate and her husband, Clark Holland. While MHT was off in New Orleans, he had quite a little cadre of Vermonters up in Coushatta running the store. This didn't go unnoticed.

No doubt about it, MHT was a savvy businessman. And a politician. As a state senator, he separated Red River Parish from adjoining parishes, making his administrative tasks easier; helped establish the town of Coushatta as a trading center on the Red River; won state contracts to do reclamation work on the levees; built a courthouse in 1872; applied business practices (like renting adjoining land to capture economies of scale) to the production of cotton and lumber; and significantly

ARKANSAS

Northwest Louisiana parish boundaries in late 1870

Map by Letitia Tunnell, reproduced from *Edge of the Sword: The Ordeal of Carpetbagger Marshall H. Twitchell in the Civil War and Reconstruction,* by Ted Tunnell improved the condition of the blacks. As long as things were going well, no one complained. Things would change. There were more acts in this play and there was more complexity in his personality.

Obviously, in retrospect, what really caused sparks to fly was not so much that MHT had imported much of his Vermont family to run his holdings, but that he had started to install them in crucial roles as tax collector, district attorney, and supervisor of registrations. Worse than his nepotism, however, was that he was getting rich, and getting rich seemingly at the expense of the long-entrenched whites. At his peak, he owned about five thousand acres of fertile farmland, some bought at foreclosure sales. No failure is as grating as the success of others, and no other is more unsettling than the outsider, and no outsider worse than the victor, and no victor as bad as the self-important one. In this sense, at least, MHT was playing his role of vice character to a tee.

Along with slowly losing the support of his various constituencies, MHT was also losing his wife, the woman who tied him to this part of the country. She had borne him a son, my grandfather, but in 1874, she died of TB. Had MHT been only an opportunistic exploiter of the beaten-down South, this would have been the time to grab the candlesticks and go north. But it's clear that with his Vermont family completely transplanted, he considered himself part of Dixie. This was home. Although he had a Yankee's distrust of what he took to be southern bombast and pretend courtliness, he clearly was putting down roots.

MHT was especially dedicated to improving race relations. He believed, as did many of his Puritan forefathers, that education was not just the great equalizer but offered the promise of a better future for all. He lived what he preached. He taxed the citizens for schools, schools for whites and blacks, and made it a point to stress that races would be treated equally, at least in this regard. MHT assured the whites that if they trashed the black schools, he would do the same to their schools. Separate but equal was okay as long as equal was achieved.

Now can we pause a moment before the bloodbaths begin? Lest I be accused of ancestor worship, I have no doubt that MHT paid more than lip service to the bromide that to the victor go the spoils. He was clearly in the catbird seat. Maybe he supported black education to some degree as a way to antagonize his opponents, but I doubt it. Maybe he countenanced a little graft on the side, cut his Vermont kin in for a little payola, padded his expense accounts, fudged on state contracts, had pork projects awarded to him because he was a senator. Maybe he raised the taxes on the widow's land and then bought it cheap at the foreclosure. Although, to the historians who have studied this in detail, such does not seem to be the case, I'm sure he was haughty and maybe occasionally had his finger in the till. Who didn't in Louisiana? Corruption is more than a tradition in Louisiana; it's the norm.

In the patois of politics, he was running what was then called a "ring," and this involved some obvious croneyism. Still, I doubt there was financial chicanery involved because I know this kind of man, this kind of Yankee. I grew up with them. They are annoying, to be sure, not because they are corrupt but because they are so cocksure of their own righteousness. It's not enough for them to outfox someone; they want to tell you about it. Worse, they want to tell the person they outfoxed about it. They are, in the terms I heard as a kid in Vermont, too clever by half.

The Colfax Riot/Massacre

So what happened? About forty miles to the south of Starlight Plantation is a small town called Colfax. On Easter Sunday in 1873, the whites decided that the blacks were getting out of hand and killed about seventy of them. Or 140, depending on who you read. You can read about this in any number of places, but please don't read the standard Louisiana textbook. This view is/was commemorated on an infamous 1951 historical marker still on the side of U.S. Highway 84: *On this site occurred the Colfax Riot in which three white men and 150 negroes were slain. This event on April 13, 1873, marked the end of carpetbag misrule in the South.*

More respectable historians like Eric Foner and Nicholas Lemann have taken to calling the uprising what it was: a massacre. And the massacre itself has recently become a stand-alone subject of considerable interest. Two books, both published in spring of 2008 (*The Colfax Massacre: The Untold Story of Black Power, White Terror, and the Death of Reconstruction*, by historian LeeAnna Keith [Oxford University Press]; and *The Day Freedom Died: The Colfax Massacre, the Supreme Court, and the Betrayal of Reconstruction*, by *Washington Post* reporter Charles Lane [Henry Holt]),

Louisiana state historical marker in front of modern courthouse in Colfax. The only honest thing about it is the date, and even that may not be entirely accurate.
Photo by author

as well as a best-selling novelization published at almost the same time (*Red River*, by Lalita Tademy [Warner Books, 2007]), have made clear that almost every single word on this signpost is a travesty. Ditto much of Louisiana schoolbook history. Not a "riot" but a massacre; at least one of the white men was killed by "friendly fire"; and the carpetbag "misrule" may have been a much more equitable system for more people more of the time than what replaced it. The standard morality-play interpretation played out by the hackneyed vice characters simply won't stand up. What happened in Colfax was a mindless slaughter of innocents by what essentially was a death squad of self-appointed vigilantes.

I'm going to tell you a bit about it because, in one form or another, this is the history that informs all of the Deep South from one end of U.S. 84 to the other. The Civil War didn't make Dixie Dixie, Reconstruction did, and much of what we know about Reconstruction is a repetitive, self-serving story of dispossessed whites battling for their hijacked rights and possessions. They just wanted back what was rightfully theirs. If only those scheming carpetbaggers had left them alone.

The elections of 1872 were furiously contested in many places, not the least in upstate Louisiana. For a while, Louisiana even had two gov-

26

ernors, both claiming patronage rights to appoint local officeholders. Blacks, who believed they had won (and they probably had since they outnumbered the whites by more than four to one), holed up in the Colfax town hall, insisting that their nominees be put in place. They believed the occupying U.S. government troops would come to their aid once the vote count was certified. They were understandably belligerent about their victory. They doubtless thought that turnabout was fair play.

Disgruntled whites didn't think so. So before the Feds arrived, the ex-Confederates surrounded the building to install their slate of officials. Adopting a chain of command and even weaponry that they had used during the Civil War, the whites proceeded to lay an orderly siege to the courthouse. They called themselves the White League, and, in distinction from the KKK that followed, they were unabashed in their public candor. Blacks had to go back to the way they were.

The Union troops didn't arrive. They had their hands full elsewhere as firestorms like this were occurring all across the South. So the White League, already in place and itching to do what they had done not so well a few years earlier, proceeded to slaughter the poorly organized and hopelessly outgunned blacks. With something like military precision, they wheeled a small riverboat cannon, a so-called five-pounder, across an embankment to the shore of the Red River and trained it on the blacks, who foolishly were entrenched behind hastily constructed breastworks. The whites filled the cannon with nails and metal shards. What happened next was like shooting fish in a barrel as the blacks were trapped between their own earthworks and the courthouse. Black ordnance consisted mainly of old shotguns and farm tools like pitchforks and shovels.

In short order, the blacks were forced back into the building, where, being surrounded, they surrendered. As some of them came out of the courthouse waving pieces of white, either paper or clothing, over their heads, they were gunned down. Their compatriots, seeing this, refused to leave the building and hid under the floorboards. The White Leaguers then set the building afire. Those who didn't perish by shrapnel, bullets, or smoke were captured. According to federal records, these unlucky prisoners numbered about forty. And finally, in what can only be described as carnival macabre, Mardi Gras run amok, these forty were exuberantly killed in the twilight of Easter Sunday.

For reasons best left to psychologists, the young white men, who did most of the killing, tortured the prisoners, adopting the language and behavior of frontier cattlemen. They called the blacks by the names of cattle —a favorite appellation is *boeuf*—killing them in a likewise manner. The killers hooted and hollered as if they were driving cows to slaughter. They kicked the blacks and beat them with sticks. They experimented to see how many human heads a bullet would pierce. Many of these youths had been too young to fight in the war. They had been left on the farm. Now they were old enough, and it seems that this butchery was their way of catching up. Elders stood by and watched. You may recall that this scene is not foregrounded in the morality play we heard about in history class.

For its size and degree of atrocity, the Colfax massacre was one of the grizzliest slaughters in history. Not only was it the worst in American history, it was on a par with anything that has happened with death squads in South America (Argentina, Chile, Peru . . .), Central America (El Salvador, Guatemala, Honduras, Nicaragua . . .), Europe (Germany, Serbia, Spain, Turkey . . .), Africa (Rwanda, Somalia, Zaire . . .), Asia (Sri Lanka, Indonesia, Philippines . . .). There is only one term for it: *genetic cleansing*. Colfax was far, far worse than Rosewood, Florida (1923), and Greenwood, Oklahoma (1921), where white mobs lynched and killed blacks. True, some Indian massacres (the Gunther Island Massacre of Wiyot Indians in 1860) and Civil War engagements (Confederate troops under Nathan Forrest at Fort Pillow in 1864) had higher rates of crazed slaughter, but those bloodbaths had tacit state support. Colfax is a marquee event in the archives of homegrown death gangs: that you may never have heard of it is possibly interesting. Neither had I. But here's the point: something like this, albeit with the carnage volume turned down, was happening all across the Deep South in the 1870s. Every little town that U.S. 84 goes through is a Colfax.

Worse, the U.S. government in Washington, D.C., had heard of it. They knew how many blacks were slaughtered, how the slaughter occurred, and even who the perpetrators were. There was a formal inquest. There was a handful of corroborating witnesses, mostly blacks who had not been killed in the schoolboy jubilation. Although there were two trials, no court edicts ensued, no one went to jail. And that's because

Gathering the Dead and Wounded in Colfax (engraving), *Harper's Weekly,* May 10, 1873
The Granger Collection, New York

while everyone knew who the killers were, the appeals went to the U.S. Supreme Court, which, like the rest of the nation, had had a bellyful of Rebel blood. Enough Reconstruction. The North wanted to be done with the South. There were too many Colfaxes. So the Supreme Court refused to get involved and essentially said that this was a matter that Louisiana should settle on its own.

And, sad to say, they knew exactly how Louisiana would settle it. States' rights = malicious neglect. Home rule = return to slavery. In fact, until the middle of the twentieth century, the national courts knew full well how the Deep South states would deal with these problems. Look away, Dixieland. They knew the Deep Southern states would countenance the rule of mobs, the rule of death squads, the rule of a Lost Cause newly found, especially when uppity blacks were involved. The North might have won the war, but the courts made sure that the South would win the Reconstruction. It was a pyrrhic victory at best. That's why *Brown v. Board of Education* and other cases addressing the Equal Protection

Clause of the Fourteenth Amendment in the 1950s were so important. They essentially said no more pretending Colfax doesn't exist. Reconstruction essentially began in the 1960s.

The Coushatta Riot/Massacre

Whew! Now we get to my great-grandfather. After the death squads had dealt with the unruly blacks forty miles to the south of Coushatta, they inspired White Leaguers to take action elsewhere—northwest to Natchitoches and south to New Orleans. Since the long arm of the law was too short to pursue the killers, why not restore the antebellum status quo? Why not north to Coushatta, where MHT and his coven of carpetbaggers were not just harassing widows and orphans but educating the blacks?

MHT had plenty of warning that he was next on the docket. In his scrapbook there is this warning note (April 16, 1873), presumably penned by one of the Colfax elders:

Mr Twitchal Sir I must inform you that in [?] weak [probably *court week*, the first Monday of the month] your Town is to be overrun and all your Nigger officers and sum of your white men are to bee killed. I was in the fite at Colfax And if the lord will forgive me for that I wil never bee gilty of such a thing agane a lawyer from your town was hear and one of your depty sherifs And the matter was all fixed the forces are too come from plesant hil and from this parrish And are to collect in differant Neybourhoods and to come on of A suddin you have men amung you who pass for frends but who are Enemys you ar in grate danger they entind to kill all the yankees and Nigger officers you had all better make your escape as men enuff will come to do the work in a few Minnits

A true frend

In his autobiography, published by LSU Press in 1989 as *Carpetbagger from Vermont: The Autobiography of Marshall Harvey Twitchell* and edited by Ted Tunnell, MHT confesses that when told Coushatta was to be cleansed, he believed that only the blacks were at risk. And he made it clear to the White Leaguers that Coushatta was not going to become another Colfax. Then, however, he went off to the legislative session in

"Note from a True Friend" to Marshall Harvey Twitchell
In possession of the author

New Orleans, leaving his appointees to deal with this bubbling brew on their own.

In retrospect, his notion that he'd be exempt from White League retribution seems a bit delusional. On the other hand, he was still being reelected by more than the black vote, and he was, by many accounts, a fair-handed albeit high-handed magistrate. In addition, MHT had been through almost twenty Civil War battles. They are all listed on his sword, the one I spent time waving about in Vermont. He had seen lots and lots of dead men lying in piles. He had almost joined the piles on at least two occasions. Why shouldn't he think he would be exempt from the fury of Colfax? Probably the most comforting thought to MHT then is today the least appealing: blacks were being slaughtered, not whites. The *white line,* as it was then called, had not been crossed.

Not yet. In the late summer of the next year, 1874, under the guise of suppressing yet another Negro rebellion, White Leaguers congregated in Coushatta, along what is now U.S. 84. This time there really was an incident. A black man, frightened by night riders who were patrolling the town while a dance was taking place, shot a white picket. The black man was hiding under the house of MHT's brother, Homer Twitchell. The wounded man appeared at the dance with blood dripping from his face. What could be more fortuitous for invoking the mandates of chivalry? Who cares if only a single black man had panicked? Purportedly to protect the perpetually at-risk women from black rape and pillage, the White Leaguers decided to gather up a few blacks. In addition, they now had a pretext to include the Twitchell cohort. What were this black man and others doing at Homer's house if not spoiling for a fight and a chance to violate women? Who was filling his mind full of salacious thoughts? Damnyankees.

The so-called minions of MHT were rounded up and put in protective custody. One brother-in-law, George King, was allowed to return home, perhaps because he was too sick to travel, or possibly because he was a high-ranking Mason. Another associate, Henry Scott, a Master Mason, was ushered out to safety. After spending the night in jail, the six officeholders were told to get what valuables they could carry, leave their wives and children (who would be vouchsafed passage later), and essentially get out while the going was good.

As a sign of good faith, the six would be escorted to safety across the parish line and, if need be, all the way up to Shreveport to the state line. In some versions, they were told that they could even choose the escort guard.

So on August 30, 1874, six of the MHT ring were mounted up and led to the northwest. They were his brother, two brothers-in-law, and three political appointees. Now, the story as it was told to me as a kid: From time to time, as they were escorted to the northwest, they could see little clouds of dust on the horizon. This dust was being lifted by horsemen coming at them from behind, maybe from Texas. Did they know they were being led into a trap, an ambush? They must have suspected.

Contemporary newspaper accounts are untrustworthy in explaining what happened next. Papers spewed the politics of either Carpetbagger (Republican) or White League (Fusion Party). MHT saved those reports in his scrapbook, and in a macabre way they are fun to read, for not only do they show the truth of the tale of blind men and the elephant, but also they show how wonderfully exuberant the writing in early newspapers could be. They are positively witty and wicked on both sides, not even a hint of objectivity. Fox News is pablum in comparison.

On September 10, 1874, the *New York Times*, prefiguring its reputation as the gray lady of journalism, carried the story under the headline "The Southern Terror: Alarming Condition of the Louisiana Parishes":

> The six murdered white men were told the day before their murder that they must take their watches and jewelry with them, as their captors would not otherwise be responsible for the safety of their property. They did so, and after they were murdered their bodies were robbed of everything that had any value. They were entirely stripped. Four of these persons were married and had families. Only one of them was permitted to see his wife. Three of them had married Southern ladies and were living there with their families. The guard who conducted the six men out to be murdered were thirty five in number, well mounted, and armed with double-barreled shot-guns. The refugees state that the White League was continually receiving reinforcements up to two days after the murder. The league is organized in companies which are well armed and disciplined, and thoroughly drilled by good officers. All the provisions in the town have been seized and preparations made of a regular siege. The person who sends this dispatch does so in the belief that no correct account of the story of these refugees may otherwise reach the North.

Oddly enough, the place to go to get the feel for what happened is a work of fiction, a novel about MHT written by a mild antagonist, Mary

Bryan. Bryan was a popular writer of women's fiction then living in Atlanta but who had lived for years in the Red River valley. Since what happened was national news, she traveled back to Louisiana to get the story. She supposedly had what the newspapers lacked: an eyewitness. Bryan got so caught up in the event that she wrote a book, *Wild Work: The Story of the Red River Tragedy* (D. Appleton, 1881), a piece of nonfiction fiction worthy of Truman Capote or Norman Mailer. She may play fast and loose with the melodrama of the overreaching carpetbagger and the innocent bedraggled Rebels (as well as the never-to-be trusted blacks, who would just as soon slit your neck as serve you a julep), but she gives what looks to be a feasible telling of the massacre.

To make sure we understand where fiction ends and fact begins, Bryan even appends this footnote to her rendition: "The circumstances of the pursuit and killing of these six office holders are given almost word for word as they were told me by one of the men who accompanied the prisoners as a guard" (315). I, for one, believed her, as did my family.

Here's her version from the point of view of one of the escort party. She gives the six men not-very-opaque pseudonyms that I've translated in brackets. I quote *Wild Work* at length because it has the smack of truth and has been the basis of the usual interpretation of what happened at the end of August 1874. Only much later, at the end of my trip across U.S. 84, did I learn of a different version, a version I now think is more trustworthy.

After the entourage has been riding for most of the morning, the horses and men are tired. They stop for a rest.

Here was a watermelon patch, and yonder, a little farther off, was a store and a cistern. We'd strike a halt and send for water and melons while the horses took a rest. So we got down. It was just beyond our parish line; I remember that, for I heard somebody say so, and Devene [E. W. Deweese, MHT's tax collector] looked quickly at Witchell [Homer Twitchell, younger brother of MHT] and seemed disturbed, but Omar [Homer] didn't seem to mind his look. He was sitting on the grass, and was pale and absent-minded. Edgeville [Frank Edgerton, sheriff] was gay as ever, but I saw him, when he had his back to the men pretending to stroke his horse's neck, take Miss Blair's [his fiancée] picture out and look at it, and his face got somber as he looked. Some of the men were cutting watermelons. Walton [Monroe Willis, supervisor of voter registration and MHT's brother-in-law] was standing by his horse, looking down the road we had just come over. Omar was telling me not to go away after we got to S——[Shreveport] without seeing him first, as he would have a letter for his wife he wanted to trust to my care, when, suddenly, Howard [W. F. Howell, district attorney, an ex-Confederate officer] cried out: "Look! see all those men with guns; what does that mean?" We turned our heads and saw a posse of armed men on horseback turn the bend in the road and come galloping up to us. Devene cried out: "Mount and ride for your lives." They ran for their horses and jumped into the saddles as quick as thought, but their pursuers were upon them. The foremost man cried out: "Surrender!" and others yelled the word after him. The mob began firing. Omar turned in his saddle, with the blood running out of a wound in his neck.

"Give me a gun; I don't want to die like a dog," he cried. The bullets rained upon him, and he fell under the horses' feet. Edgeville cried out: "I'll die before I surrender." He dashed ahead and reached the top of the hill; a bullet struck him in the head; he leaped up out of his saddle and fell to the ground dead. Devene was killed at the same place. Wallace and Hollin and Howard got some distance away, but they were caught and taken to Bard's [Ward's] store a mile or so beyond, and there put an end to. Howard was shot first. The old man trembled like a leaf. He got down on his knees and begged them to spare him. Wallace, too, prayed to be spared. He said: "God is my witness, I have never done a wrong to any man in this country. I am only a magistrate. Witchell [MHT] sent for me here to superintend his business. He gave me a home in his house and this office. I have held the office only a little while. I have tried to do what was right."

They shot both of them. I counted the places where ninety buckshot had entered Howard's body. Mark Hollin stood and saw them shot. When his turn came he said: "Let me say a prayer." They suffered him to kneel down, and he prayed in silence a little while. Then he rose up, and said, calmly, "There is only one thing I ask of you; that is, for God's sake don't harm my wife and my little child. Let them go away in safety. That is all." He was so cool and brave they stood with their reloaded guns in their hands as if they thought it almost a pity to kill him. As they were going to shoot, a man galloped up and cried out: "A thousand dollars if you will spare the prisoner's life!" They turned on him and he said: "I don't make the offer myself; I do it for another man. He's got a fall from his horse back yonder, and he's not able to come on. But he's got the money, for I know him. He said he'd give a thousand dollars of every life you spared, and I am only in time for one, I see."

Some cried "Humbug!" and some "Plank down your money; let's see the color of it!" and several cried out to Mark Hollin to run into the cotton-field, they'd give him a chance for his life. But he stood still and said: "You have killed all my friends, now kill me. I will not run for my life." Well, they shot him. I went up and looked at him. His face was as calm as if he had dropped to sleep. I don't know what they did with the bodies; I went away. I felt sick and numbed, as if a bullet had entered my own head. The looks of those dead men will never get out of my mind. As I rode back and passed where the others were lying, I saw one of the men taking off Edgeville's watch and chain. . . . I saw one man taking out the diamond stud-buttons from Mark Hollin's shirt—the same his little boy told me he had put in. I couldn't help feeling awful bad about the wives and children of the men, who were praying and hoping they were safe, while they lay there dead. They deserved to be punished, I know, but it looked like a bad day's work. (313–15)

So the tally was this: Homer Twitchell, Deweese, and Edgerton were killed first while trying to escape; Howell was shot on his knees, followed by the murder of Willis, and Holland was shot last standing still. Clearly, the *white line* had been crossed and crossed and crossed.

In New Orleans, MHT soon got telegrams describing what had happened. He went first to the governor and then to the U.S. Fifth Circuit Court, which appointed him a U.S. commissioner, granting authority to investigate, issue arrest warrants, organize posses, and even travel with a small army escort. Meanwhile troops of the Seventh Cavalry (later off to Custer's Last Stand) were dispatched, arrests were made and suspects jailed, but prosecution proved fruitless because, as Colfax had shown, the state was unwilling to follow through.

For the next two years, MHT made desultory trips back to Coushatta, but with no real enforcement power, it was feckless. So he essentially reburied the dead, tidied up business, took custody of his two now-orphaned nephews, and tended to his mother and his only son, my grand-father. When he disinterred the graves of the six victims, he found, just as author Bryan had said, the corpses perforated with bullets. But he also found what she did not report: that the private parts of one (unnamed, but it probably was his brother Homer) were mutilated (as reported in Ted Tunnell's book *Edge of the Sword: The Ordeal of Carpetbagger Marshall H. Twitchell in the Civil War and Reconstruction* [LSU Press, 2001], 225).

But what could he do? He had no enforcement power because, as Colfax had shown, the U.S. government, like the state of Louisiana, had had a bellyful. Plus, insurrections like this—not as bad, but gruesome nonetheless—were occurring across the Deep South, in Alabama, in Mississippi, and in Georgia, many along the line currently traversed by U.S. 84. In almost every downtown square or on a courthouse wall you can still find a little plaque or reminder not that the war had happened but that resurrection had happened. The charade of Reconstruction was coming to an end.

MHT certainly knew that the chaos was pandemic. New Orleans it-self had erupted in what was the largest street brawl in American history in which 3,500 White Leaguers faced 3,600 police and black militia. (As with Colfax, it too was immortalized in the 1930s as the Battle of Liberty Place, complete with an obelisk commemorating the event that "gave us back our state.") Still, MHT didn't leave Louisiana. For more than a year, he essentially commuted from New Orleans to Coushatta under armed guard, took care of what was left of his family, and tried to keep his plantations in business. They certainly needed his attention. They were in steady decline. He decided not to stand for reelection.

The Assassination Attempt

Still, the townspeople of Coushatta must have wondered what part of *Get the hell out of town!* MHT didn't understand. They decided to up the ante. At the end of April 1876, my kinsman returned to Coushatta, en route back to Starlight Plantation, and was surprised to find a number of his old political opponents milling around the dock. When MHT asked why the late meeting, he was told there was some town business that they were trying to resolve. In a few days, he would find out what that business was.

Here now in his own words:

> On the morning of May 2, I started for Coushatta with Mr. King, the last of my Northern brothers-in-laws and the one who had escaped assassination two years before on account of his serious illness at the time. As we stepped down to the river and took our places in the skiff, the negro ferryman urged me not to cross that morning, but I was so accustomed to negro timidity that I disregarded his advice and ordered him to pull for the Coushatta shore. Just as we were about to touch the bank I looked up from the paper which I was reading and saw a man standing behind a woodpile leveling his rifle at me. I called out, "Down in the boat," and the first shot went over us; then to the ferryman, "Pull back to the other shore." The next shot passed through the skiff and entered my left thigh. I immediately went over into the water, passing under the skiff, and caught hold of the lower edge with my hand, keeping the skiff much of the time between myself and the assassin, while all the time I was partially concealed under the boat and in the water. King, having a revolver, fired two shots at the assassin and was shot dead. One shot at him or me shot the ferryman in the hand.
>
> The assassin was one of the coolest of the kind which the South ever produced; and as a marksman, he was an expert, using his repeating rifle and revolver with such rapidity and accuracy that notwithstanding the poor mark I gave him by the time I had reached the middle of the stream, he succeeded with his last rifle shot in shattering my remaining arm, and I floated on my back away from the skiff. He then fired two shots from his revolver, the last one striking my coat.
>
> Apprehensive that more might follow and hit my body next, I told the ferryman to call out that I was dead. This he promptly did, the words being repeated by ladies on the shore, and the assassin cooly and leisurely mounted his horse and rode away.
>
> The ferryman brought the skiff on the lower side of me, I threw my only uninjured limb on the edge of the boat, and the ferryman, with his unwounded arm, rolled me over into the skiff upon the body of King. (Autobiography, 170–71)

As with the violence in Colfax, Natchitoches, Coushatta, and New Orleans, this event would be investigated but not prosecuted. What the Forty-fourth Congress in Washington, D.C., learned in its interrogation (*House Reports*, 1st sess., no. 816, quoted in Tunnell, *Edge of the Sword*, 241) was that the gunman had arrived that morning, left his horse at the town blacksmith shop saying he'd be back later, scoured the riverbank looking for a good spot for a straight shot, and then patiently waited. He attracted some attention, as well he should have. For he was wearing a black slouch hat pulled down tight over his forehead, a false beard, green eye-goggles and a long oilcloth coat. I pictured him looking rather like Darkman from the superhero comic book.

When Darkman spotted the skiff leaving the far side, he ambled back to get his horse and then slowly rode to the woodpile on Front Street. He dismounted, pulled a sixteen-shot Winchester from the saddle holster and, holding it near his right leg so it couldn't be seen by the men in the skiff, went to the riverbank.

Then he did his business, the business he had probably been contracted to do by the deadlocked city fathers MHT had seen only days before. He shot my great-grandfather in both arms. A few uninformed townspeople made the mistake of approaching while the grisly deed was being done, and he waved them away with his pistol. The goggled, hooded, fake-bearded, trench coat–wearing man said he was just doing a little alligator hunting. When he calmly returned to his horse, sheathed his rifle, and mounted his steed, keeping a cocked pistol in hand, he seemed in no hurry. In fact, as he calmly rode out of town in a scene worthy of an upside-down Shane, he was asked by a black servant woman if that was really an alligator, and he replied, "Yes, it is a damned black alligator."

Who was he? No one knows for sure, but he may well be the same "Captain Jack" (in real life Richard Coleman, no kin to Adele Coleman, and a well-known desperado) who may have led the band of killers in the earlier Coushatta slaughter. Or, as I was to learn later, he may have been a local homeboy, a White Leaguer who was known to the Coushattans and protected by them. Maybe he was chosen by drawing lots. After the deed, he went to Texas to lie low. Once President Rutherford B. Hayes granted a general amnesty, the morality play was over, and he came back and lived out a quiet life.

MHT reported in his *Autobiography* that he later learned there had been some hard feeling between the assassin and his employers because this recent job had been botched. The town fathers did not want to pay up. Supposedly the gunman himself had had some remorse, saying, "If I had shot the damned nigger [ferryman], I should have got him [MHT], as he would have sunk before anyone could have reached him from the shore" (*Autobiography*, 173). As I was to learn, that street-talk gossip may have been a ruse to protect the gunman.

No matter, while the assassination may not have succeeded, the desired ends were met. In weeks, MHT, both arms amputated, finally realizing he was not wanted in Louisiana, made his way back to Vermont to remarry and care for what was left of his family (which wasn't much: two orphaned nephews, a son, and his mother). He had plenty of time to run the tally of his life in Deep Dixie: two sisters dead of yellow fever; two infant sons dead, one in childbirth and the other in infancy; a wife dead of tuberculosis; a brother-in-law shot to death in the ferry crossing; a brother and two brothers-in-law killed in the Coushatta massacre, and a sister who died of exhaustion en route back to Vermont. In the years between 1873 and 1876, he lost ten family members and his right and left arms.

MHT was hardly the triumphant carpetbagger made famous in cartoons, lugging his ill-gotten swag back to Yankeeland. He had no hidden family farm in Vermont, no secret Canadian bank accounts, no cache of pilfered Confederate candlesticks. True, he kept some of Adele's jewelry, but other than that his carpetbag was empty. That is not counting all the paper memorabilia.

Wisely unwilling to return to the Coushatta courthouse to contest his Louisiana property rights, his plantations fell into the hands of rapscallions, who contended he hadn't properly purchased them. Nonsense, as court documents attested, but MHT was not about to return nor make yet another claim that he couldn't enforce. Thanks to a little "jury nullification," the land steal was done on the legal up-and-up. There was a bona fide jury verdict.

MHT returned to Louisiana only once, not to Coushatta but to New Orleans, to finish out his term in the senate and, in so doing, to cast a crucial vote for Hayes, thereby breaking a deadlock and resolving the disputed national election. Earlier in 1877, Hayes had traveled to Newfane,

Vermont, and the two men had spoken. What did they speak about? Was there a deal, a quid pro quo? Probably. The two national parties came to a secret compromise: southern Democrats agreed to accept a Republican in the White House, and northern Republicans agreed to abandon Reconstruction. MHT must have known what this Compromise of 1877 really meant—the selling out of the freed slaves and the delivery of amnesty to their tormentors. But there were not many job openings for a man with no arms. MHT was given a sinecure by the incoming administration. He became the American consul in Kingston, Ontario, where he lived out his days in mild neglect. He died at about the age I am while writing this. He often complained that he was bored.

Understanding a Morality Play

It's one thing to tell a story. Sometimes it's an entirely different thing to understand it. And still more confusing is that sometimes the same story can be understood in totally different ways at different times by different audiences. In the first part of the twentieth century, the story I've told was interpreted in the South and some of the North as: "Carpetbaggers got their just desserts." This interpretation was made popular by newspaperman Horace Greeley (carpetbaggers "are fellows who crawled down South on the track of our armies . . . stealing and plundering"), historian William Archibald Dunning, novelist Margaret Mitchell, and filmmaker D. W. Griffith. Carpetbaggers from the North and scalawags from the South exploited the exhausted Confederacy, leeching off what little was left, and then went away pocketing the change. Raise taxes, pounce on the Confederate widow's land, skedaddle back north. The moral of the play: good riddance. The hero of the play: southern Everyman.

Then, beginning around the 1960s, historians (inter alia, John Hope Franklin, Otto Olsen, Lawrence Powell, Richard Current, George Rable, Eric Foner, and Ted Tunnell) took a different view, perhaps a view informed by the general realization that the vaunted *states' rights, noble cause,* and *southern honor* might be better understood as meaning, "Gimme back all my stuff, including my slaves." Suddenly, in one generation, the morality play of Reconstruction was turned on its ear, and many of the roles and much of the action were reinterpreted.

What precipitated this change in the story was, among other things, the rising role of African Americans. In the old-style version, the southern yeoman was considered to be the Everyman; he was the put-upon commoner who was elbowed aside by the scheming carpetbagger. In the new version, a once minor character was foregrounded, a character who had been essentially invisible in the earlier versions—the newly enfranchised black. Perhaps as the civil rights movement sent Yankees south for a second time and saw blacks often killed and then bodies covered up (flickers of *Mississippi Burning*); perhaps as blacks saw what happened to those among them who lobbied for change, and perhaps as southerners themselves looked seriously around and asked, "How did this mess happen?" the meaning of some stories changed. The black man came stage center. The southern melodrama of the poor, woe-is-me, put-upon South became a morality tale of the evils of a culture enthralled to slavery. Not by happenstance does this shift in narrative focus occur during the real Reconstruction, the so-called Great Society of LBJ.

Not to put too fine a point on it, but as the role of blacks changed (think Kunta Kinte in *Roots*), the stoic southern plowboy often became the ineffectual redneck blowhard (think *Hee Haw, Beverly Hillbillies*, Sheriff Buford T. Justice of the *Smokey and the Bandit* movies, and the raft of comedians from Jerry Clower to Jeff Foxworthy). As this happened, the historical drama of Reconstruction was reconfigured. The carpetbagger was off the hook; the shortsighted southern bigot became a vice character. Who could have lived through the mid-twentieth century and not been impressed by the likes of Lester Maddox, Orval Faubus, George Wallace, Bull Connor, and the young versions of Strom Thurmond and Jesse Helms? They didn't come off a soundstage in Hollywood. They were real.

Since the Great Society generation, MHT has become something of a poster boy for the admittedly conflicted but generally positive reinterpretation of carpetbaggers. In each retelling from the first piece done in the 1960s to the most recent ones, including a 2003 PBS documentary called *Reconstruction: The Second Civil War,* MHT has become more the sympathetic reformer for black rights and less the money-grubbing exploiter of Confederate widows in the demoralized South. Many of his putative flaws are now seen as gutsy behavior.

Now, just as my dad predicted, I've become interested in my kinsman

Captain Twitchell. Some of my interest is personal. Here's why. In my family, whenever anyone didn't express emotion, we'd say, "Well, whatdaya expect, how can you learn to hug in an armless family?" My dad used to eat milk toast on cold Sunday nights. When I asked him why, he said that it was a favorite of his grandfather. For a while I was confused, thinking that my great-grandfather had something to do with being a milquetoast. But it was because milk-saturated toast could be slurped. MHT couldn't cut his food, and so he was hand-fed pap for most of his later life. His family was served the same mush food he slurped: Welsh rarebit, chipped beef on toast, corn bread soaked in maple syrup. So were we.

I'm also curious about this: my great-grandfather intended to leave Vermont and settle in Louisiana. Some of my die-hard Yankee relatives don't believe this, but I don't doubt this for a second. MHT brought his entire family down from Vermont not so he could rape and pillage the locals but so he could re-root his family in the South. He married a southerner. He was investing his life. He was not filling up his carpetbag with goodies to take back north. He had plenty of chances to leave. In other words, at some level, my great-grandfather wanted me to be a southerner. If he had been left alone, I might well have grown up along Highway 84. He had sunk the Y axis.

And certainly part of my interest in my great-granddad's story is cultural. What happened in the 1870s, that bloodshed, those scenes of slaughter and mayhem, played out in a particular place, the Deep South. No other region of North America has experienced homegrown, state-sanctioned, stand-alone death squads slaughtering their own people. These were more than lynchings; these were out-and-out massacres. And the gore runs all the way across the land traversed by U.S. 84, from Waycross to the blood-soaked banks of the Red River—the X axis. The blood has long since dried up. What remains? So here's another question: Is there still a scab, or, to be more polite, can you see in the pentimento of current culture the trauma that was Reconstruction? Did it make the south the South? Is this the true heart of Dixie? How much of the turmoil of yesterday can be understood by looking carefully at the surface of today?

So these are my two story lines: one in the here and now (the X), the other in the long ago and far away (the Y). How much of the same ground do they cover? If one is geographic, literally covering the ground from Waycross to Coushatta, and the other historic, covering the time between a defeated South and its perceived reformation, do they touch at any points? Is culture both today and in history, through space and time, in events and memory, seen and felt? Was Faulkner right when he wrote, in *Requiem for a Nun*, that "The past is never dead. It's not even past"? Or, to write it with a travel agent's crayon: Does the deep past live in the shallow present? Can you travel across space to go back in time? Do some roads go out and down at the same time?

2

March across Georgia

O public road . . . You express me better than I can express myself.

—WALT WHITMAN, "SONG OF THE OPEN ROAD"

O
n January 20, 2009, the day of President Barack Obama's inauguration, we started our exploration of Dixieland by driving the View up into the Okefenokee Swamp. My wife and I
were going to spend a few days getting acclimated to our land yacht at
the Stephen C. Foster State Park. As we learned, that's a few days more
than Mr. Foster ever spent in the entire state of Georgia. His song extolling being "way down upon the Swanee River" was composed way up
north in New York. He had never set eyes on the Suwannee River, which
empties this swamp, carrying its dark red water down to the gulf. If you
want to understand how the North created the South (at least before
Hollywood took over), there is probably no better place to start than in a
swamp. In many respects, the swamp is at the edge of the X axis, at least
as perceived by Yankees. Ground zero, literally, zero ground.

I wanted to start our trip in a swamp because, although it seems obvious when you think of it, before all else, the Deep South is wet. And a
century ago it was a lot wetter. In fact, it was sopping wet. So, like Marlow in *Heart of Darkness* when he arrives at the African shore, we needed
a staging area before heading off looking for MHT, our Kurtz. Our river
of asphalt, U.S. 84, headed out along the north edge of this swamp into
the unknown Dixie. Like the Congo snaking its way up to the unknown

jungle, U.S. 84 was going to take us all the way over to Coushatta, where unspeakable and perhaps unknowable acts had occurred.

The hoary metaphor of road as poetic river was not hard to come by. For almost the entirety of our trip, the highway was literally made by dredging the sides of the road and then building a causeway. Water was almost always beside us, just over the shoulder. We knew when we were coming into a real swamp because the water level in the ditch would get closer and closer to the level of the road. When the sunlight was just so, the gray road and the reddish ditch water glistened a dull russet. Every twenty miles or so, there was a gleam of microwave antennae above the green horizon of pines. It didn't take much to imagine I was on that puttering steamboat upstream heading out past the buoys into the Unknown.

My plan was to go from Okefenokee Swamp in Georgia to Grand Bayou in Louisiana. These are both mushy places and in many ways the opposite of the world of New England. The world MHT and I came from was hard, rocky, steep, and cold; the world he and I were going into was soft, moist, flat, and warm.

Admittedly, the Okefenokee is the extreme. It's a liminal place, not really ground, not really water. It's porous and oozy and there is no sense of support, let alone habitability. This is especially true at night. The stars high above are brilliant; there's no ambient light from human settlements. The sky is filled with soap bubbles for stars. The wet earth is perpetually coiling and uncoiling at the same time; everything is living and dying simultaneously. The deep swamp is living hell for an agoraphobic, not a hard edge in sight. There are no markers, no towering peaks, no horizon, nothing to set your compass by.

Until recently, you couldn't successfully drain it. After all, one of the great communal endeavors of the pre–Civil War days was to attempt to pull the plug on the Dismal Swamp to get at the rich bottomland. Even George Washington couldn't do that. Yankees looking for apt images for southern culture found it here in the swamp: corrupt surface, fertile underneath, and undrainable.

Still more propitious for Dixiephobia is that all the chief American swamps are in the South: the Great Dismal is in extreme southeastern Virginia, the Everglades are in south Florida, the vast Atchafalaya is in

Louisiana, and the Okefenokee is along the Georgia-Florida border. Oke-fenokee is what the Seminoles called the Land of Trembling Earth. And the land literally trembles because often it's not land at all, but a big mound of floating mud-goo. From time to time, big air bubbles trapped in the goo explode with a huge burp that can literally shake the ground.

Had you crossed Dixie with my great-grandfather, it would have been so much swampier. In his day, it was dripping wet, much closer to a jungle. As Ann Vileisis reports in *Discovering the Unknown Landscape: A History of America's Wetlands* (Island Press, 1997), at the turn of the eighteenth century about half of Florida and Louisiana was vast swampland; between 25 and 50 percent of Mississippi and the Carolinas was soggy; and between 12 and 25 percent of Georgia and Alabama was so viscous you couldn't walk across it without sinking in. True, geography may not be destiny, but it helps.

By the time of the Civil War, some soggy land had been drained to satisfy King Cotton's appetite for loamy earth, but hardly a dent was made. The real destroyer of swampland came after the war as lumber barons, mostly from the North, came looking for yellow pine and cypress. Thanks to them, more than 200 million acres of swampland dwindled to 99 million. They built the drains and laid the railroad track not to farm crops but to harvest timber. Then they planted jack pine for pulp, for paper and newsprint, so they could tell their tales of Dixie.

When you think about it, the swamp is such a powerful cultural construct; it lies at the heart of the northern creation of the Old South. Easy to put your foot into the mud blubber, hard to get it out. Easy to go into a swamp, but hard to escape. It's gassy and abysmal, stained with tannic acid, quicksand around every corner. You are not going to meet anyone companionable like a kindly woodcutter or a yodeling guide in a swamp. When I told my Yankee friends I was going to be driving across the Deep South, they often started to hum the banjo piece from James Dickey's *Deliverance*.

People who live in swamps are weird and dangerous. They are demented trappers, crazed Indians, mulattos, swamp maroons, and criminals on the lam. They drool and play an important role in our adolescence, coming out of black lagoons, promising to do terrible things. They spend a lot of their time at witches' sabbaths. They breed among themselves. That all having been said, Pogo ("we have met the enemy and he is us") lives in a swamp, as does Shrek. Go figure. Maybe the only good swampers are cartoon characters.

As you know, our first day deep in the Okefenokee was the day of Barack Obama's inauguration, so maybe all the confusion was serendipitous. The swamp/black man combination may seem whimsical, even nonsensical, but historically, and tragically, there is a fit. American swamps have been safe harbors for runaway slaves, at least in our imaginations. You don't see many black men standing confidently on the Capitol steps

Runaway slave hiding in a swamp
Courtesy North Carolina State Archives

In the Swamp, lithograph by H. L. Stephens, c. 1863
Library of Congress, Prints and Photographs Division, LC-USZC4-2522

Fugitive Slaves in the Dismal Swamp, Virginia, David Edward Cronin, 1888, oil on canvas, 17 x 14 in.
New-York Historical Society

taking the oath of office. But the image of the black man, up to his waist in swamp muck, peering out from overhanging branches, was a central nineteenth-century trope. He is one of those people who can survive the swamp.

Is this why the black man is safe in the swamp? Because it's a terrible place, but better than the alternative? That the slave in the swamp is protected by exactly what the white man fears: the sucking powers of uncontrollable nature, may tell us something of our racial imaginations. The black man can live in this black loam. After all, what's the heart of Africa but a vast lagoon of black mud?

And this muck wasn't simply a visual cliché; it's all through American literature. Think of Longfellow's "The Slave in the Dismal Swamp" (which is about exactly that); Stowe's *Uncle Tom's Cabin* (escaped slaves populate the swamps that surround Simon Legree's plantation); and Twain's *Huck Finn* (after the raft was hit by a steamboat, Huck finds Jim deep in the goo, afraid of being tracked by dogs, but safe).

This imagery usually comes from the North. The folks who settled New England had a rich history of swamp anxiety that may come all the way from England. Recall the Beowulf creature who comes up from the ooze to harass humans, that the Christian Everyman in *Pilgrim's Progress* almost gets stuck in the Slough of Despond, that Milton's devils inhabit an area like the Serbonian Bog, and that Dickens describes the slime below London in *Great Expectations* and above the ground in piles of wet garbage in *Our Mutual Friend*. England didn't have vast swamps; neither did New England. Aside from tidal estuaries, there is not much true swampland in either England or New England; bogs, fens, marshes, yes, but massive never-ending swamps, no. Maybe that's why the swamp was so important in northern pictures of southern life.

Southern Swamps Filled with Northern Meaning

Here's my point: humans cannot think without images, without analogies, without metaphor. And the swamp was one of the central ways the North dealt with the South. The swamp is the *other* culture, the unconscious miasma. It's what lies beneath. For Freudians, maybe it's the id. From William Bartram (*Travels*) to Melville (*Pierre* and *The Confidence-*

Man) to Poe (*Fall of the House of Usher*) and even to openhearted Whitman (*Leaves of Grass*), the swamp is something to be carefully circled, possibly never entered, always redolent with decay, maybe death.

I think it's quite unconscious, which makes it all the more powerful as an assumption. The South as swamp never has to be questioned because it's never discussed as such. To the city on the hill, this is the culture in the bog. It's the opposite of terra firma, moral purity, and fixed purpose. Essentially, the reason the swamp was in the South is because only the Old South, the Deep South, Dixieland, had those undercurrents of ooze, depravity, slavery, sin.

Without overthinking it, Charles Eliot Norton, that archetypical patrician Yankee, opens up what the southern swamp meant to the northern imagination:

> The miasma that broods over Carolina in the summer seems to me but the emblem of the invisible, unrecognized, blindly guessed at moral miasma that rests over the lands where slavery exists. If I ever wrote against slavery, it shall be on the ground not of its being bad for the blacks, but of its being deadly to the whites. The effect on thought, on character, on aim in life, on hope is . . . plainly as sad as anything can be. (*Letters of Charles Eliot Norton* [Houghton Mifflin, 1913], 1: 121–22)

Everyone in the North knew the South was sopping wet, sucking in every living thing, a surface with no substance, a gummy maw. The war proved it. Few in the North did not know about the quagmire General Burnside was caught in during his march to Richmond in 1863. And who, as the war continued, didn't know about the vast suckland around Andersonville devouring more Yankee prisoners than starvation? And by the end of the war, all northerners knew about the never-ending Atchafalaya around New Orleans. From one end of Dixie to the other it was all the same: a morass that entraps the unwary.

I certainly don't want the quivering swamp to carry too much weight other than the obvious: the swamp is something to be leery of, stayed out of. No one was more responsible for constructing this view of the South than Harriet Beecher Stowe. Even Lincoln knew that. In her bestselling novel *Dred: A Tale of the Great Dismal Swamp*, written right after *Uncle Tom's Cabin*, the swamp is a sanctuary to runaway slaves, but a blood-sucking vampire to slave catchers. It leaches the bloodlife of all nasty whites who dare enter. And what makes this particularly on point is that Stowe had never seen a southern swamp when she penned this antisouthern screed. What she knew was the power of topography to unsettle the mind. Old South = swamp = bloodsucker.

You can't stay in the Okefenokee Swamp for long without being swamped by how things have changed. The swamp is now our savior. In fact, like the good darkie and the minstrel in motley, the southern swamp (as created by the North) has been sent to the museum, or at least to the EPA.

Like the other players in the morality play called *Reconstruction*, the swamp has come in for a change in makeup. Perhaps as the North finally made peace with the South in the mid-twentieth century, the American swamp disappeared and *wetlands* took its place. Along with a new name came a new analogy. Instead of the miasma came the filter, instead of poisonous reptiles came the wildlife refuge, instead of nature-out-of-control here was the control-for-nature. The swamp is now seen as the vast gauze purifying the poison of the world *outside* the swamp. The swamp is regenerative, edging out the waterfall as the image of cleanser, the strainer of putrefaction and recharger of the aquifers. No longer a force of rebarbarization, breakdown, and devolution, the wetlands offer salvation. Id becomes superego.

Ruskin and the New South

After a few days, we emerged from the swamp cleansed, ready to hit the road. Victorian journeys usually started in harbors or train stations (think Jules Verne, Ernest Shackleton, David Livingston), and modern ones often start in bars (road novels) or airports (Hollywood films begin with the landing gear retracting or descending). With the exception of Pogo's and Shrek's brief excursions, I can't think of one journey that starts in a swamp. Ours did.

Driving up out of the swamp, whoops, wetlands, and turning northwest to U.S. 84 into Waycross, Georgia, you go through a blink of a town called Ruskin. All you now see is ramshackle house trailers tinged in rust, a discount liquor store run by a member of the India/Indian motel/ Patel clan, and some somber one-story churches. Each church has the requisite recycled school bus festooned with painted daisies, flecked yellow paint, and the church name splashed on the side. The only claim to fame that this section of U.S. 84 has is that here begin two Seaboard Coastline rail tracks that run diagonally across the state, so straight that the WPA guide claimed this as the longest stretch of uncurving railbed in the entire country.

U.S. 84 runs perfectly parallel to these tracks, a tribute to the flat bed of wet earth that made such great cotton fields a century ago. The land was ruined after thirty years of intense farming. By the 1840s had begun the slow trickle of farmers looking for new fields, cutting the path now taken by us.

In the southwest corner of the town across these tracks is a beautiful little Victorian shingled church called the Old Ruskin Church. The town was named for John Ruskin, the great Victorian art critic and social reformer who caused such a stir in the 1880s by not just upholding the values of honest work but by defining work itself the cause of human contentment. Ironically, it was only after the Industrial Revolution that someone could actually make a case in favor of sweat labor with a straight face. Contradicting Adam Smith and those dismal market

The Old Ruskin Church, Ruskin, Georgia
Photo by author

economists who said that labor was just a cost of doing business, Ruskin made work the reason for business. More than anyone, he coined the term *honest labor.*

In a series of letters addressed to workingmen later published as *Fors Clavigera: Letters to the Workmen and Labourers of Great Britain,* Ruskin blew the trumpet of the Arts and Crafts movement: machine-made = bad; handcrafted = good. He gave the Luddites intellectual heft: work is a religion of sorts, and anything that belittles work, such as mass production, contract by union, or payment by the hour, belittles not just the human condition but the will of God. The machine, presumably even the cotton gin, is sacrilegious. So how the hell did he get to Dixie?

Here's how. The late nineteenth century was fertile ground for back-to-basics voluntary simplicity movements, and here Ruskin fits right in —a kind of vulgar communism for the common man without all the pretense of Marx and Engels. What were called "Ruskin Co-ops" became, along with places like Brook Farm, Fruitlands, the Oneida Community, and New Harmony, a reaction to machine-made objects, factory-subsidized towns, and alienated laborers.

How this communitarianism fit into the Reconstruction of the postbellum South is revealing, because this kind of cerebral and articulate reaction to the Industrial Age was far more common in New England. The South had no tradition of Fight the Machine. What machines did they have to fight, aside from the cotton gin, which after all, was an unalloyed benefit? Slavery was a machine of a different sort, as was sharecropping. Southern gentry abhorred sweat, and *honest labor* was an oxymoron. So the response to planting a Ruskin Co-op along U.S. 84 in the 1890s may tell us a bit about the social flexibility of the South.

Or, more specifically, it may tell us about the adaptability of what became known as the New South. This term was coined by Henry W. Grady in a series of articles and speeches as editor of the *Atlanta Constitution* in the 1880s to describe a South chastened by the North and eager to enter the marketplace. Grady was to begin a refrain line that continues to this day. When you hear people talk of the histories of Charlotte, Atlanta, Memphis, Orlando, and even New Orleans, you'll hear how this is the *New* South. And how it portends the end of Dixieland.

Historically the New South was not mindless Babbitry, but the restoration of the agrarian South, the restored-to-colonial-days South, the slavery-free South. *New South* was self-consciously used to displace the term *Old South* and all that that stood for—SBC (South before Cotton). In this sense, Grady's New South was what was defended in the 1950s by the writers associated with Vanderbilt University in the 1930s (Donald Davidson, Andrew Nelson Lytle, John Crowe Ransom, Allen Tate, Robert Penn Warren) in their important collection of essays called, with heroic passion, *I'll Take My Stand*. What it really was was SBS—South before Slavery. And as such, it forms a provocative counterpart to the much more violent restoration of prebellum days that was occurring in places like Colfax and Coushatta, Louisiana.

So how did this New South find an outpost along U.S. 84 in Ware County at the turn of the twentieth century? While Grady was announcing that the SBS South Would Rise Again in the late 1880s, an Indiana newspaperman named Julius Augustus Wayland was founding a newspaper—the *Coming Nation*—and predicting that the workingman would rise again. Wayland started a cooperative community in Tennessee—Ruskin Cooperative Association—cribbed on Ruskin's exhortations to workers, to give it an intellectual boost.

Here's the argument. Human work is honorable regardless of task as long as it fosters the commonweal. Hoeing a field is like caring for the sick which is like teaching a child which is like building a barn. It's not how much you earn; it's how you earn. Since your work was as valuable as your neighbor's, having different wages insults both of you. There should be no premium on danger or complexity or even drudgery when the ultimate goal is cooperation. All should be paid equally in a common currency of community value in which literal coinage was just a lubricant.

The newspaper was a big success if only because no other community was providing such a play-by-play description of what it was doing to the assumptions of market capitalism. People were curious. The *Coming Nation* not only made money; it made converts. For a while it had some sixty thousand subscribers in every state of the Union. Mary Harris Jones, the labor and community organizer called "Mother Jones," was not just a fan but a contributor. *Mother Jones*, the barely surviving present-day magazine, is, in a sense, a direct descendant of the *Coming Nation*.

In the first Ruskin Cooperative Association, squabbles over legal and personality issues arose, and Wayland quit in a huff. Looking for fertile fields to reconstitute the community—a new place without the old memories—the Tennessee members considered the New South. The weather was ideal, and the ground was not entirely worn out. Plus the railroad network, reestablished after the war, meant better distribution of the newspaper. The town name—Waycross—asserted this; it was a junction of two rail lines and three roads. Best yet, there was a budding community of so-called New Settlers already in place, in a little commune called Duke, Georgia. The Ruskinites decided that was the place for them, the land of milk and honey where distractions would be kept to a minimum. Honest labor would redeem Dixie.

In an act of PR bravado, the Ruskinites rented an entire train, and 240 members piled their stuff on. A separate car carried all the printing equipment. They made their very public way down into the New South stopping for interviews along the way. Pictures were taken. Local papers ran the story. Hopes ran high, even though a child died en route. The

Arrival of refugees from the Ruskin Commonwealth, a utopian community in Tennessee, at Ware County railroad station in Georgia, 1899
Courtesy of Georgia Archives, Vanishing Georgia Collection, war 002

Ruskinites chugged the 613 miles to their new home right up next to the Okefenokee Swamp, just off U.S. 84.

No doubt about it, they were a curious lot. For all their caterwauling about the sanctity of labor, they were more than willing to employ the economies of mass production. Along with publishing the newspaper, they made and marketed leather suspenders, chewing gum, a cereal-based coffee like Postum, and, most successfully, brooms made with cornstalks. They were also an intellectual lot. They had debating societies, reading groups, a library of more than a thousand volumes, a light opera theater, a nine-month school complete with a full-time professor, and a traveling troupe with a band that entertained on the road. They were always proselytizing. They even had a ten-room hotel for the curious and the dabblers.

And they were also contentious. *All for one, one for all* makes sense when there are only three musketeers, but when there are more than two hundred, intense community can pressurize and crack the group. And indeed it did. The winter of 1901 was unseasonably chilly, the crops didn't come in, and since everyone was living close together, when one person became sick or cranky, everyone was at risk. Likewise, all their buildings were either connected or adjacent. So when the coffee plant burned, it consumed part of the living quarters. In more ways than one, they were living too close together. Ruskin was too intimate.

But the real troubles, as one might have predicted, were in the master plan. Was labor really fungible? Did all honest work equal all other honest work? Isn't some work more important than other work? Aren't some jobs just donkey labor? What's so redemptive about sweat? Ironically, this is exactly the assumption that the Old South was based on. Slavery depends on it.

The Ruskinites learned the hard way. If a broom maker goes to sleep on the job, isn't it different than if a typesetter takes the day off? And there was endless bickering about how to charge fees to enter the group. For a while it was almost five hundred dollars, but at the end you could join with a sawbuck. What should have shown them the error of their ways was that right from the start the newspaper types, who were bally-hooing the nobility of work, were being charged less to enter. Forget the wage squabbles; this should have told them work was not interchangeable. There were always money troubles. Was there graft upstairs? Seems so. And then the inevitable problem: sex. Familiarity doesn't necessarily breed contempt, but it almost always breeds trouble. If things were genuinely communal, well, you know the rest of that story.

The Ruskinites were goners. They were barely able to last two years in the New South. After the first year, membership dropped by half. But here's what I think is telling. They collapsed from the inside out. Other groups in New England went bust because the outside townspeople couldn't put up with shenanigans like, say, the free-love antics of John Humphrey Noyes and the Oneida community. Who but the transcendently gullible believed in his teachings of "Complex Marriage" or, better yet, "Male Continence"? And how come these doctrines were always coming from holy-but-horny middle-aged men? The growing Church of Latter-Day Saints membership was regularly harassed and even pursued by neighbors. The Mormons were wise enough to pick up sticks and keep moving west. But the sign of distress at Ruskin was that many of the families started to take their meals not in the community room but in their bedrooms. There was no place to move to. They were right on the edge of the swamp. Mired.

Southerners tolerated the Ruskinites even though their worldview was antithetical to that of the Old South. But the neighbors didn't have much curiosity. The Ruskinites came out into the community to seek converts, but they didn't return with many members. Ruskin's ideas weren't appealing to Dixie; the idea of intense community, the idea of taking chances with inherited forms, the idea that work itself can be reconfigured, the idea that there's no intrinsic social hierarchy—the list of opposing views was long. Call it southern stuck-in-the-muddiness or eyes-wide-open to silly social schemes, the local interest was nil. But so was local hostility.

The reason the Ruskinites were left alone was because they had absolutely no truck with the blacks. There were no black members, and there was no intent to recruit blacks. Interestingly enough, after a few years of such communism-lite, the local black sharecroppers were probably living better than these high-minded, big-thinking neighbors. For a while, Ruskinites were living on about nine cents a day. They were becoming enslaved to an idea whose time had not yet come.

The Ruskin Commonwealth was effectively disbanded in the autumn of 1901. Some members went back north, some commuted into Waycross, and some moved along U.S. 84 to a little community west of Valdosta called Kinderlou. The land was sold and became a sawmill and turpentine factory, the printing press went to a newspaper in Florida, large sheets of newsprint went to wallpaper nearby sharecropper houses, the broom handles were made into fence posts, and the books went to form the initial holdings of the Waycross–Ware County Library.

We drove all around what was once the community. We walked over the places the buildings had been. Like the world seen by the poet in Ozymandias, "Nothing beside remains. Round the decay . . . boundless and bare / The lone and level sands stretch far away." Well, not sand but swamp.

And one more thing that makes this informative about the South. We could find no one in Ruskin who knew any of this history. It's as if it didn't happen. And the same is almost as true in Waycross. One local woman wrote a master's thesis on the community in the 1930s. We went to the Visitors Center; they had never heard of it. And to the local newspaper. Not much interest here, although a retired writer had been curious enough to write a piece on the experiment. In fact, we only knew about the noble experiment because those WPA writers in the late 1930s thought that this was important enough to include in their guide. They were clearly intrigued for the obvious reasons. Ruskin was an ideal writers' colony. Sitting around scribbling was as important as pulling a plow or pulling up weeds.

After Ruskin we became doubly curious about what the South can and cannot absorb. Clearly a commune based on the principles of Marx, free-for-all religion, and possible free love can get in. But a community of Yankees who might educate the blacks is kicked out. Ruskin made the cut; Coushatta did not. Now I realize that it's much more complex than that (Ruskin was apolitical, for starters), but still the general subject of *what stays, what goes* became a focus of what we were to see along U.S. 84.

Some of my prejudice about southern prejudice was mistaken. I realized that the South is tolerant, in many areas far more tolerant than is the North. Southern hospitality is for real. Their arms are open. But what seemed to separate the South was this exquisite sensitivity to a social hierarchy based on oppressive nonsense. Here it would brook no dissent. As the twentieth century was to show, such nonsense is all the more powerful precisely because of its irrationality. Think the last days of Weimar Germany. It can't be argued with because it has no counterargument. Racial prejudice achieves the condition of unquestioned belief. At this point the arms close. Outsiders must leave.

The Decorative World

Right down the road from Ruskin was the first of a multitude of junk stores that stretched all the way across U.S. 84 to Louisiana. They were not just on the outskirts of many towns but in the centers. They seemed to be the only suppliers of objects that could compete with the omnipresent Walmart and Super Walmart, and the Super-Duper Walmart that is doubtless to come.

This one, called the Bargain Depot, was just an old home stuffed with washpots, colored pop bottles, syrup containers, ammo boxes, and mounds of spilled utensils. From the road the Bargain Depot seemed to be cascading its wares of rusting farm machinery and large black cane-cooking pots out into the road. Clearly, this was some of the stuff that stayed. The only things printed on paper were a few farm magazines, no old copies of the *Saturday Evening Post* or *Life* magazine. And no books. Hard life needs hardware.

As well, there was little decorative matter, the kind of stuff that hung on walls or that was placed on tables. This was a culture devoid of the competitive parlors of New England. When I asked John Lewis, jovial proprietor and inveterate collector, if he had any decorative follies, any knickknacks, anything whimsical, he showed me a chicken made of plaster and an upside-down bottle with a narrow throat that hung on the wall. Did I know what it was? No idea. A flycatcher. But even that was functional. I bought the chicken.

If the material world can be trusted to tell us what people value, then this was a rough world, a barely-hanging-on world, a world too concerned with survival for indulgences, and a world in which the Ruskinites didn't have a prayer. With the exception of the quilts of Gee's Bend in Alabama and one wood-carver outside the town of Ringgold, Louisiana, we didn't see what are called the decorative arts—the stuff someone sells along the road like pottery or baskets.

I remember reading somewhere that one of the reasons that decorative crafts flourished in northern latitudes is that families had to come inside from the freezing cold, essentially hibernate, and that they carved and wove objects as a way to pass the time. Families and tribes traded secrets and competed in their nonutilitarian handiwork. The South had no killing frost, no snowbanks at the door, and hence never had long stretches of desultory time. They had this swampland and this brutal summer heat. There was no respite, no bleak February, no time to hunker down, in a sense, no privacy.

All the way across Georgia we could see how tough the life must have been. It hadn't changed much since the WPA writers had passed this way. What they saw, we saw. Margaret Mitchell and Hollywood notwithstanding, there wasn't a Tara in sight. Cotton was long gone. Even the endless forests of yellow pine that had once provided plenty of timber and what were called naval stores (turpentine and rosin) had disappeared. Pulp wood was now the crop, the plantation owner was a paper company headquartered in Manhattan, and the farmer was in a doublewide. With ships turning to iron, cotton turning to chemical fabrics, and peanuts moving to flatter land to the west, this part of Georgia was in a time warp. The primary crop seemed to be microwave antennae growing in the front yards and huge cell phone relay towers growing in the fields.

What's a Yankee Worth?

And things continued this way all the way past Valdosta until we reached Thomasville, a small town just north of Tallahassee, Florida. Thomasville proved a still better lesson in *what gets in and what is kept out.* While so many in the Deep South railed against Reconstruction, while so much of the culture along U.S. 84 dedicated itself to what it called *Resurrection* (the violent return to a culture based if not on slavery then on Jim Crow domination), this little colony in south-central Georgia took a chance and threw open the door. Thomasville is the anti-Colfax, the South without Reconstruction.

Oddly enough, Thomasville had a strange affinity with Waycross. They were both willing to try new things, to let new people in. Thomasville, however, was a bit more picky. The *Thomasville Times* in August 1900 even carried this observation occasioned by a rosy column in the *Waycross Herald* on how its Ruskinites were doing: "The Colony of Ruskinites near Waycross is living on 9 cents a day and they are living well, too. Perhaps can't you send us a receipt for this kind of living?" (quoted in Larry Purdom, *By the Way: It Happened in Waycross* [Brantley, 2005], 1:70). The comment is sardonic for a reason. Thomasville was experiencing a slightly different crop of newcomers living on a slightly higher allowance.

Thomasville's experiment with allowing outsiders in started a little sooner than Ruskin's. Here's what happened. In 1860 there were 6,244 slaves; 4,488 whites, and 34 "free persons of color" in Thomasville. Of the 403 slaveholders, 50 owned one slave and most owned fewer than ten slaves. A large population of yeomen farmers owned few if any slaves and were nearly self-sufficient. That was about standard for central Georgia. As with Waycross, its citizens had participated in the Civil War, maybe not with the zeal of coastal Georgia, but without the antisecessionist temper of parts of the mountains. They put in a presence, showed the stars and bars, fought the fights, and later built the war memorials to prove it.

But for reasons that no one was able to tell us, there was an unusual amount of racial amity after the war. Was it because there were no carpetbaggers? No Twitchell and his pack of conniving Vermonters? Maybe. Perhaps it was a function of the railroad, because a spur was built in the 1860s South from Albany down into the piney woods. The plan was to collect the naval stores for the war effort, but its real war function was to ship prisoners down from Andersonville (near Albany) when it was feared that Sherman was on his way to liberate the prison. Sherman had other hell to raise and moved eastward instead.

What the railroad ended up doing, however, was to deliver a different genus of northerner into those loamy woods to be rusticated, not incarcerated. Thomas County was as far south as one could travel by rail, and by the 1880s, just two decades after the war, thousands of Yankees were congregating here for the winter season.

By the turn of the century, when snow fell in the American Midwest, Thomasville's population exploded. The snowbirds landed. It became the Miami of its day. In the matter of only a decade, about fifteen hotels were built, a few of them patterned on the grand hotels of the Catskills. Two of these hotels even had their own orchestras. For three months of the year, time was kept in terms of costume balls and galas. There were boardinghouses all over town, and soon "cottages" in the manner of Newport appeared along Dawson Street. This Yankeefication would all collapse when the swamps of northern Florida were drained, mosquito populations controlled, and train tracks finally laid down on the eastern coast. By the time Henry Flagler rode his Florida East Coast Railway into Key West in 1912, it was all over for southwest Georgia. But until then Thomasville was indeed grand.

Thomasville never had the *forget hell, forgive never* southern animosity toward this Yankee intrusion. In fact, they exploited it. The anxiety about racial tension had been overwhelmed, or at least sublimated, by money. Some people I spoke to attributed this to the fact that when the town ran short of funds to bond the railroad construction, the "freed men of color" made the crucial financial contribution. As well the town had united to move an underfunded black normal school from nearby Quitman, which improved the quality of black education in Thomasville. (Perhaps by happenstance Quitman now has a store on the main drag selling Dixie paraphernalia—"Proud to be a Redneck" over the Rebel flag on T-shirts and shot glasses.) In terms of *what stays, what goes,* Thomasville as a southern community was able not just to do well but to do right.

Even after the bottom fell out of the Yankee-thawing business, Thomasville prospered. Large plantations were bought by some of those same families who had earlier come to the hotels. Now they came by private railcar and built hunting preserves. Dressing up to go foxhunting replaced dressing up to go waltzing. In the 1920s, the generation before the graduated income tax, the scions and scionesses of middlewestern fortunes spent their time currying horses, pampering dogs, polishing silver, shooting birds, and chasing foxes.

We went to one of these plantations, Pebble Hill, the home of some of the Hanna family, which made its fortune in mining, railroads, political corruption, and especially Standard Oil. Characteristically, the big house is not patterned after the antebellum plantation but after an English country house. The Hannas took the picturesque squirearchy of Capability Brown and Alexander Pope and plunked it down here, complete with grottos and gazebos. They had no interest in the Old South. The inside of the mansion looks like an explosion in the Paul Mellon collection of art. Every single room is chock full of heroic horse and noble dog. It's even in the wallpaper and on furniture.

Perhaps it's a parody of Anglophilia and grouse hunting, but Pebble Hill in particular and Thomas County in general gives the lie to southern xenophobia. These Yankees were welcomed. When I asked one of our guides how this little county had been able to prosper while the surrounding counties seem suffocating in comparative poverty and racial resentment, I was told with a smile that the unofficial motto of Thomasville is, "A Yankee is worth about two bales of cotton and easier to pick."

Southern Pantomime Violence

When I had planned my trip along U.S. 84, I'd checked with the State of Georgia tourism bureau and told them of my interest in the culture of the Deep South, withholding mention of my curiosity about bloody massacres. They suggested attending either the Swine Time Festival in Climax or the Rattlesnake Roundup in Whigham. Alas, Swine Time had come and gone—it's the first Saturday after Thanksgiving—and by the time we'd be motoring through, Miss Swine Time would have been chosen and best hog caller known. So it looked like the Rattlesnake Roundup for us.

Friends from Vermont, Jon and Louise, joined us for the festivities. Jon was an aficionado of poisonous snakes, having almost been bit by a rattler the size of a moving van some years ago in Arizona. I promised southern warmth necessary to get the rattles rattlin', but the day was really chilly. No self-respecting snake would be venturing forth on a day in which he could see his own breath. But no matter. We pulled up to the fairgrounds in the RV—a large marquee sign out front announcing *The Rattlesnake Roundup*—and were ushered into the pecan trees to park. Plenty of RVs around. I was with my people. But I was already anxious about the serpents underfoot. I was high-stepping lightly.

This was an old-style country fair; it had been going since the 1940s. There was no farm machinery, no livestock to judge, no vegetables to coo over, no 4-H exhibits, but there was plenty of stuff to look at while awaiting the snakes. And most of the stuff did have a reptilian theme. For instance, you could buy a stuffed rattler in the springing position holding a light fixture for your dining room table. You could buy a stuffed armadillo with a circular spot between his feet to put a beer bottle. Even the fairgoers participated. There was a middle-aged woman dressed as a snake with shiny leotards and snakeskin jacket.

The roundup was not all snakes and snake paraphernalia. You could buy a hat with nifty sayings on it like GAP (the small text explaining, God Answers Prayers); a T-shirt proclaiming, "I'm going with Jesus"; a grain of rice with your name engraved on it (very small); some jewelry made from nails in the shape of the cross; a large choice of knives, some the size of sabers; and then, from an Asian man, two entire tables of *genuine* Coach handbags.

And there was the usual inventory of Dixieana—the Confederate war flag on various garments with appropriate sayings about how Rebels never forget and how the South could be counted on to rise again. There was also a collection of engraved belts, inscribed T-shirts, and suitable-for-framing pictures of Barack Obama. This line was long and entirely African American.

The Ecumenical Snake

The snakes were the main attraction, and in this genuinely integrated crowd we all stood in a small amphitheater to marvel at, in a sense, the anti-Christ. There's a famous saying from Martin Luther King Jr. that the most segregated time in America is 10 a.m. on Sunday morning, and I suppose he's correct. We may take our savior separately, but the devil we take together. The Rattlesnake Roundup was as salt 'n' pepper as we were to get prior to boarding the gambling boat in Natchez. Getting scared and being fleeced are two events that know no color boundary.

As in a morality play, the snakes entered stage right. Carried in by thin, white middle-aged men (not a black man in any of the groups of snake hunters), the snakes remained unseen in their large brown boxes.

The men were wearing camo, tan hats, snake boots pulled over pegged jeans, and a look of weariness. Bits of their families trailed behind. A few of the snake men carried long aluminum poles with a little hook at the end. A disturbing number seemed to be walking with a slight limp. They opened the boxes and carefully lifted the snakes and dumped them into large garbage cans with a kind of devil-may-care attitude that gave the crowd the audible shivers. They were essentially shoveling these snakes around. From time to time they'd look into the garbage can and pull out a particularly big snake and dump him into a galvanized tin can to be weighed, and sometimes they'd dump one out on a table to take his measurements in public.

Finally, they hooked the biggest snakes in the garbage cans and cast them into large aquarium-like boxes. One of the black men near me in the audience said that's to warm the snakes up so they'd behave properly. And they needed the jolt. They looked so tired, just hanging there limp on the stick.

But then I had to ask myself why were the snakes being moved into the garbage cans; why not just pour them into the aquarium boxes in the first place? It was, as I was to later realize, because it was all part of the show, a show that these snake handlers had been doing for quite a while. Every time we saw a snake being picked up and moved in front of us, our hearts raced. Often the handlers would walk the snake all the way across the ring, giving us the heebie-jeebies. What if the snake should fall to the ground? We didn't have snake boots on.

We didn't have to wait long for that to happen. A snake would accidently fall off the hook and the crowd would rush backward. You could hear the young girls squeal the retreat. The somnolent handler would come alive and pick it back up and continue the transport from container to container. After a while I noticed that the dropped snake really made no effort to slither away. The poor thing was too cold to make tracks. Not us; we were continually moving around.

While all this snake transportation was happening, a scholarly man looking much like Wilford Brimley was peering at the various specimens. He wore red suspenders. His work station was down in front, near the middle of the crowd. It was a Plexiglas altar with a glass funnel attached to a quart jar. Willard would go up to one of the aquariums, examine the snakes, pull out a slumbering giant with a pole, and then, in a flourish, he'd swing the snake around so that he held its mouth in his right hand and caught its tail under his left arm. Then he would squeeze on the snake's jaw, and we could see little squirts of milky stuff go into the funnel and down into the container. He would unceremoniously drop the exhausted snake into one of the garbage pails. There was something sexual about it, no doubt.

Over the loudspeaker we were informed that Wilford was none other than Ken Darnell, CEO of Bioactive Inc., a major supplier of much-needed rattlesnake antivenin to the free world, the assumption being that without men like Ken, our boys in Iraq would be dropping like flies. Snakes are all over the Middle East, weren't they? Plus that milky stuff would be used in research for finding various blood thinners. One called Integrilin had already been found. Bioactive was leading the way. And so, just by being here, we were helping by supporting much-needed research.

Then Ken took the microphone and proceeded to give us Rattlesnake 101. The rattlesnake is a pit viper; it can only strike about half its length and only from a coiled position; it usually strikes only to kill but will strike to intimidate. In that case, it won't inject poison. Hence when it strikes a human it usually doesn't spit the poison. We also learned that the female is bigger and more enthusiastic about the intimidation process since she has her kiddies to protect. Your car keys are your best defense.

The crowd is rapt. But this last factoid has us all confused. What does this mean? Ken is comforting. If bit by a rattler don't suck out the poison—chances are it's not there. Use the keys. Drive to the hospital. Whew, we all feel better. The snakes are measured, and they are big (about seven feet long), and heavy (about eight pounds); the winners announced, prizes awarded, and then, as far as I could see, the snakes are put back in those wooden ammo boxes and taken back to the pickups.

I must say I was jealous of Ken. He knew how to teach this class. And the more I thought about it, the more obvious it was that I was watching an ancient drama. In the earthen amphitheater we confronted the objects that attract our repulsion; alluring things that could cause us death are brought before our gaze. In came the totemic anxieties, carried by special porters. The objects of fear were delivered to the priest/oracle, he rendered them poisonless, passionless, milked them dry, and then returned us to the world with the knowledge we needed. It wasn't clear what happened to them. This process is, after all, the basis of religion: exaggerate the fear, provide the surcease. Comfort the afflicted, afflict the comfortable.

After a little research on the Internet back in the RV, I learned that the Rattlesnake Roundup was pretty much a sham. There are about thirty such roundups a year, mostly, but not all, in the Deep South. They have begun to cause groups like the ASPCA and PETA to rattle their own tails. That's because, as Ken himself admits, rattlesnakes are not really dangerous, especially now that most farming takes place in air-conditioned tractor cabs and very few people get bitten. In fact, these snakes that were purported to be rounded up locally have come from far away because the indigenous snake populations have been decimated. So the snakes we were seeing were being used over and over, not returned to the wild or turned into snake steaks. (Some were sold at the roundup as barbequed filet-o-snake, but we were too late, thank goodness.) Worse, these snakes are caught not by wily trapping but by shoving a garden hose down a gopher tortoise hole and pumping in a little gas. This annoys the rare tortoise and renders the hole uninhabitable for other animals. The snakes come limping out and all but crawl into the burlap bags. In other words, the snakes we saw being shoved back into the boxes most probably were just going down the road to the next roundup.

Most upsetting, however, was the venom that Dan was collecting was not going to save our boys in the desert. The FDA has strict rules, and no U.S. producer of antivenin would purchase venom collected at a roundup. Venom degrades rapidly when exposed to air, and the little collecting vial was open all through the show. Schering-Plough, the manufacturer of Integrilin, proclaims it does not purchase any venom for its anticoagulant from roundups.

In other words, what I was watching was a flim-flam. But it was cousin to a hustle I had seen before. Years ago in north Florida I became interested in pantomime violence of a different sort, small-time professional wrestling. This was before wrastlin' was totally hijacked by the cable television antics of Vince McMahon and the WWF, when local impresarios would gather some unemployed football players and tour them around the Southeast. I used to go to Ocala, Florida, just south of me, and watch the charade of good and evil in a local high school gymnasium.

I knew I had seen this crowd before, the same mix of white and black, the same rapt concentration, the same explanation by ring announcer of the parts to be played by the various performers, and the same outcome. Rattlesnakes rounded up and destroyed? Doubtful. Wrastlers throwing chairs at each other and promising dismemberment? Probably not. Who cared if they reappeared a week later in Waldo, Florida? The one thing I noticed about southern wrastlin' is that the charade was never played out racially, never good white/bad black or vice versa. That would have been too explosive; instead it was American versus foreigner, and you can guess where those foreigners were from. Violence yes, interracial tension no. Here in southwest Georgia the show was the same; it was just country boy versus snake. More than a hundred years ago the intruders were for real and the violence was not pretend. Carpetbagger as snake.

Back up at the edge of the hill that formed the crest of the little amphitheater were the little stands selling the Bowie knives, stuffed armadillos, toy guns, hissing snakes, Obama T-shirts, and deluxe handbags. The stand that had the longest line, and it was a line that stretched out for about a hundred yards, was for Longhorn chewing tobacco. Young ladies in tight T-shirts were giving out free samples to young men in tight jeans. My friend Jon observed that these shreds of cured leaf were far more dangerous than the viper fangs. Maybe Ken's pantomime violence wasn't so bad; after all, it was just for show.

Y'all Are Rude and We Are All Ignorant

As we prepared to leave Georgia, we started to hear about a peanut factory in Blakely, Georgia, that had been producing a startling amount of salmonella. People were getting sick all over the country from the paste extrusion they produced in their rat-infested factory. Some were dying. I was intrigued; here was a subject I wanted; an example of Southern Dereliction, at least as reported by the northern media. The wire-service stories always mentioned that the noxious paste was coming "from a plant in Georgia."

So we swung a few miles off U.S. 84, with my wife reading the story on the Internet, especially as it was covered in northern papers, by happenstance, the *Minneapolis Star Tribune*. Here was the New South as perceived by the Old North. We didn't find the toxic vitriol in the news stories but in the letters to the editor. Numerous letter writers wrote in to say that they had been in the South and this is exactly what was to be expected: dirt and contagion. There is the right way (the northern way) and the wrong way (the southern way). The comments didn't seem fair to me, but I certainly recognized the Dixiephobia. When mad cow disease was found a few years ago in the state of Washington, did these Minnesotans say this was typical of the Northwest?

When we drove into Blakely there was a huge peanut-processing plant right in the center of town. But it was not the offending plant; it was one run by the mellifluous Birdsong Corp., not the nasty Peanut Corp. of America. The town looked so quaint with its city square, county courthouse, and old buildings selling the stuff that Walmart couldn't carry. There were also the requisite check-cashing and sending-money-back-to-Mexico slots in the wall. As well, there was a monument to the peanut on the town green.

I couldn't just lean out of the RV cab and ask, Where's the salmonella factory? To ask that, we were going to have to settle down and make friends. The Early County Museum was just the place, and we went inside. The museum was in an old soda-pop bottling plant and was filled with cast-off farm equipment, coonskin hats, spinning reels, cap guns, Timex watches, yearbooks and autographed footballs from the local high school. Some of the farm equipment I didn't understand (stuff to make cane syrup and turpentine), but everything else was part of my childhood.

A grandfatherly eighty-year-old man was eager to show us around the front of the museum, while in back, against the wall, a passel of women were at their computers logging in all the objects. It was clear that they took pride in their town, this was all their stuff, and their camaraderie was going to make it even more difficult to ask about the notorious Peanut Corp. and its poisoning of innocent America. But our guide was more than forthcoming. Once he had told us about turpentine and cane syrup, he told us about how awful Reconstruction was, about how the Yankee carpetbaggers came in and jacked up the taxes, and how once they had bled the county, they were kicked out. His parents remembered this. Were there any killings? He didn't know. But there was a lot of shoving around, and the South finally delivered the last shove. What about blacks? The Yankees weren't interested in them. They only wanted that land-tax money.

Then we talked about peanuts. He told us where the plant was, how dreadful the town felt about the whole mess, how losing fifty jobs was difficult for such a small town, and how tiring it was to have the endless television and news crews cruising the streets. Yankees, I said smiling. Yup. I didn't mention that Peanut Corp. of America was a southern company with a long history of serious sanitation issues. At the door he said it was nice having someone to talk to about what life was like in the olden days.

We headed out to Industrial Avenue and the factory. We had expected a parking lot full of TV trucks with rooftop dish antennae and bunches of reporters with steno booklets in hand, but no. There was no activity, only a short note pasted on the front door announcing the closing. We guessed the news window had closed for the day.

We wanted to see something, anything, and so across the street was the Early Cotton Gin Company, and we turned in the gravel driveway. A woman was driving out, and we asked if we could have a look around, and she said, certainly, just go to the office and ask for George. She was his secretary. We did. George was a man of about fifty and the plant manager. I told him of our conversation with his secretary, and then I said, "I'm sorry to be bothering you. I'm taking a trip across the Deep South along Route 84. I'm a Yankee and I don't mean to be rude . . ." and before I could continue he interrupted with, "Yeah, Yeah. Y'all are rude and we are all ignorant." Then he broke into a big smile.

Although he couldn't have known it, this was exactly what we had been thinking: that this salmonella debacle next door was typical of what happens when the South does something that takes sophistication. Of course I had conveniently neglected such matters as credit default swaps, global warming, industrial pollution, depleted energy supplies, faraway wars, inequitable taxation. . . .

We had the grand tour, a tour that could never have been given in any factory in the North. No insurance company would have allowed it.

And no plant foreman would have volunteered to do it. We followed the cotton from the wagons, up into the drying bins, down into the whirling gins, and then over into the compressing and binding machines. At every step George would stop the machines, reach in and grab the cotton and show us what was happening. The ginning part was a little scary because there were thousands of whirling blades slicing the fiber to extract the seeds. I wondered, but didn't ask, if we were getting this tour in part because the poor citizens of Blakely had been bombarded by the rat-a-tat publicity attack on his next-door neighbor.

We left with two baseball hats emblazoned with "Early Gin Company" and a miniature cotton bale. I kept thinking about how gracious he was, how Blanche DuBois' famous line "I have always depended on the kindness of strangers" depended first on living in a culture with kind strangers. Southern hospitality was as real as southern violence. How were they connected? When we drove back into Blakely there was a Fox News truck from WAGA channel 5 in Atlanta. An attractive young lady was standing beside the truck with a microphone in hand. I knew why she was in town. I glowered at her, conveniently forgetting that two hours earlier we had entered Blakely for precisely the same reason.

Sewage Happens

The next morning as we prepared to break camp in the Kolomoki Mounds campground, I did my morning chore of emptying the sewage from the View. This entails driving the rig to a dump station, attaching a large rubber flexible pipe to an outlet on the underside of the vehicle, and then opening a valve. Whoosh, out it comes, down the pipe it goes. The same people who euphemize the RV renamed the sewage: it's called *black water.*

The station was at the top of a hill, and this campground was famous as a sacred burial site for the Kolomoki Indians. Not many people stay here as it is off the beaten path, far away from even U.S. 84. But like most all the other Georgia state park campgrounds, it is centered around a small lake and is in pristine condition.

I turned the plastic pipe into the opening on the underside of the rig, thought it was fastened tightly, put the other end of the pipe in the hole for waste, and then opened the "black water" valve. You can hear the sound of sewage churning in this pipe as it goes around the corners to the hole. Suddenly I heard a splashing sound and saw that the pipe had come apart at the attaching joint. The pipe had come loose from the rig! Gallons of raw human sewage were spilling out all over the roadway and now slowly flowing down toward the pond. For reasons known only to God I didn't panic but quickly closed the valve.

I don't like to use the words *beyond words* but I must. This was not just sewage but *my* crap. And it was flowing down a public roadway in full view. I couldn't yell out to my wife, who was inside the rig doubtless doing the morning sudoku. I mean what would I say? All I could do was to open the water tank in the rig and send as much freshwater down the hill as I could, hoping it would at least dilute the sewage. There was a hose and well water at the dump station that is used to clean up whatever small mess you may have made, so I sent this water cascading down the hill as well. When I got back into the View, I couldn't bear to explain what had just happened. *Shit happens* seemed to cover it, but it didn't seem right. I just wanted to pin a note on my shirt acknowledging my affiliation with Peanut Corp. of America and be done with it. We were out of Georgia, not a moment too soon.

What had I seen in Georgia and how was it preparing me for what I knew was ahead in Louisiana? I wasn't sure. In fact, I was a little panicked. Maybe this *quest travelogue with a touch of historical interpretation* was going nowhere. Maybe the X axis was a dead end. Maybe I should have stayed in the library. Maybe it's easier to predict the future from the past than to understand the past from the present. To put a turn on Santayana's "Those who cannot remember the past are condemned to repeat it," maybe those who cannot understand the present are condemned not to understand the past. How had crossing this state from Waycross to the Chattahoochee River helped me understand the slaughter of my kinsmen, as well as the massacre of 150 blacks in the 1870s? I knew that Deep South Georgia wasn't home—those swamplands, the lack of curiosity, the plain style of presentation, the male attraction to danger and maybe to violence, the hardscrabble life, and the background presence of black people everywhere, almost unnoticed, made me a little uneasy, but certainly not anxious. I felt I was in a slightly foreign country, that's all.

In fact, if I had to admit what was the most striking (and destabiliz-ing) aspect of my trip so far, I'd have said it was the open-faced helpful-ness of everyone to me, a twanging Yankee hanging out of an RV with Florida license plates. Here was a willingness to talk to someone you don't know, and aren't supposed to like, and to make them feel welcome. A southerner could spend months in Vermont and New Hampshire and never feel this kind of politeness. So maybe they were smiling with their fingers crossed. Maybe they were really sharpening their knives behind their backs and planning a little midnight massacre. But if the examples of Ruskin and Thomasville meant anything, it seemed opposite of what I had expected. The South was not a sealed-off nation, not now and not at the end of the nineteenth century. Maybe it didn't welcome the Ruskin-ites with open arms, but it certainly didn't hinder them. And certainly the rural culture in the piney woods around Thomasville was down-right friendly. Clearly, there was something in Reconstruction I wasn't understanding, something that would turn these good country people ferocious, something that would make them want to kill more than the snakes.

3

Sweet (Almost) Home Alabama

I draw the line in the dust and toss the gauntlet before the feet of tyranny,
and I say segregation now, segregation tomorrow, segregation forever.

—ALABAMA GOVERNOR GEORGE C. WALLACE,
1963 INAUGURAL ADDRESS

As we drove into Alabama I sensed something change. It looked as if we had dropped into a new chart with new coordinates. I felt dispirited. This place was rough. There was more trash on the highway, less pride of ownership in the places we saw along the road, more sense of a grind of unremitting poverty. Stars didn't fall on Alabama, junk did. From Dothan to Enterprise to Opp, it framed the road. Mary made up a poem:

> The novelty of poverty is slowly wearing thin
> The only way to compensate is a double shot of gin.

I was more philosophical. I contributed: Do you believe what your eyes see or do your eyes see what you believe? I had predicted mid-Alabama, the heart of the Heart of Dixie, was going to be harsh—maybe that's why it was. But she trumped me. This place was bedraggled. And only gin would set us free. Forget philosophy. But the gin we favor—Bombay Red Top—was nowhere to be found. That's because the state liquor bureaucracy decides what can be stocked on the shelves, and this brand of gin is apparently verboten.

A Country Boy Can Survive

We learned about Alabama from gin. Here's what we found: there is a state liquor store system, and then there is a parallel market of private package stores. The package stores charge a bit more, and they can carry only what is mandated by the liquor commission in Birmingham. One private storekeeper, black, told me she simply goes across town to the state store to buy her replacement supplies. She smiled as she said this, aware of the nonsense. And she said I'd have trouble buying Bombay Red Top in the entire state. She was right.

As far as I could see, this duplication was a way to keep the liquor stores separate and almost equal. The private package stores seemed to be in poorer neighborhoods. No one would admit this, and again maybe it's my own prejudice at work, but the private stores serve the blacks and hence keep the state stores white. It's *Plessy v. Ferguson* applied to booze.

Not all was lost. We had purchased a Garmin GPS device to help us find our way. I didn't think we were ever going to use it since I was dedicated to sticking close to the X axis of U.S. 84. Our major interaction was to change the voice from American female to English male. That's because my wife found the woman, I think she's called Garmina, especially grating when she announced, "Recalculating." She sounded like a pouty Valley girl suffocating the last syllables to make it seem that we had made yet another mistake. Since we were making quite a few mistakes en route to package stores, we changed the voice to BBC English. The English dude we called Cecil, and his tone of voice was far more forgiving.

Cecil's forte was that he could find liquor in Alabama. If you asked someone in the street, as I did, you often heard an answer like, "Don't know; don't care." I heard that at Walmart outside Dothan, Alabama, which was disturbing because if I had to work there liquor would be on the daily schedule. But if you asked Cecil for a package store, he'd find it even if it meant you had to cross the tracks and enter a world you might have otherwise passed by.

There just seemed to be little esprit in central Alabama, at least as we entered it from the east. Everything seemed tuckered out. It needed to be ginned up. Somehow this was typified by what was dotted in the splatter of bottles and Styrofoam on the roadside: hundreds of signs imploring us, "Don't Litter. Keep *Alabama the Beautiful.*" Many signs were pock-marked with bullet holes. If ever there were an argument for a bottle-return bill, it was here. Ditto the outlawing of fast-food Styrofoam. (Well, and maybe gun control too.)

I had originally planned to stop every day at, say, two in the afternoon and spend fifteen minutes or so picking up road trash. I thought I might be able to say something profound about Deep Dixie by examining the roadside detritus. There's a thriving subspecialty in cultural anthropology called garbology, and I had read William Rathje's *Rubbish! The Archaeology of Garbage.* The gist: we are what we throw away. But the entirety of U.S. 84 in Alabama seemed a bottomless midden thick in automotive heave-ho. I couldn't get it out of my mind that in New Zealand there are no trash baskets in national parks. You are just expected to know what to do: pack it out yourself. Here it seemed just the opposite: if you've got it, dump it. Was it in part because prisoners, mostly black, used to pick it up? For a long time these prisoners were in chains. Alabama famously reintroduced roadside chain gangs in the 1990s, but the courts told them to quit it.

We didn't see many of those cloying road signs proclaiming, "This section of road is being cleaned up by so-and-so," that litter roadways elsewhere. In fact, what made this thick litter a bit perplexing was the in-your-face flying of flags, symbols of pride of place. I don't mean just the Dixie stars and bars, but the big, big stars and stripes. The American flag was waving over everything: foreign-car dealerships, Baptist churches, BP gas stations, shopping centers, and in front of many, many residences. This may seem a picky thing to ask, but what is the discon-nect between pride in nation and pride in neighborhood? Or is it simply that abstractions are easier to keep clean than realities?

Promised Land: Jews in Dixie

Although I had planned to spend some time in Dothan, we arrived on Saturday and that made my excursions difficult. I had chosen a Dothan stopover for two reasons: it once had a professional wrestling outfit that serviced the Deep South with pantomime violence, and it once had a thriving Jewish community that made it a retail/religious hub.

These may seem like different services, but not for me. They addressed a central question of my trip: What gets into the South and what is kept out? I know from family experience what is kept out (or better yet, thrown out like trash); so what is allowed in?

Plus, I thought that Dothan had a great history, a history that the WPA guide to Alabama spent some time explaining. The town used to be called Poplar Head, which referred to some poplar trees that surrounded a glade at the head of a spring. Indian trails met here and went off in several directions. Then the Christians came and in 1885 changed the name to Dothan, which was a town mentioned by Joseph in a Bible verse, Genesis 37:17—"For I heard them say, let us go to Dothan." Downtown at Millennium Park is a ten-foot-tall cast-bronze sculpture of Joseph saying exactly this. (As we learned, he's no competition for a shimmering golden statue of a peanut in front of the Visitors Information building.)

Christians or not, Jews, mostly from central Europe, poured into the South before and especially after the Civil War. By all accounts (the best is Eli Evans's *The Provincials: A Personal History of Jews in the South*) they were accommodated, even welcomed. All through the world the Jew is the archetypical carpetbagger, but not here. Here he was given safe passage. Was this because Jews fit into a culture where people had their place and could be counted on to stay put? From planter to slave/sharecropper there was an expected chain of trade, and the Jews became part of the downtown-shopkeeper category.

In almost every town we visited there was a Jewish department store and often a Jewish-named town block. Some of the more enduring remain today: Kohl's, Stein Mart, Helig, Maas Brothers, Belk's, Abrams . . . Go into any downtown crossed by U.S. 84 and you'll often find two distinctly marked and still-named buildings: the Jewish department store (empty) and the Masonic Temple (almost empty).

My buddy from graduate school, Bob Cohan, who would join us in Monroeville in his vintage Airstream trailer, had already given me the heads-up on both these temples. He said it was simple: in the ante- and postbellum worlds there was no social slot in the mercantile world for *black commerce.* Trading with blacks was precisely what the Jewish peddlers were willing to do. And the whites were more than willing to have them do this. The two groups simply had different versions of what was *unclean.* In earlier days, plantation script and the commissary kept the concept of trade away from the blacks. They "bought" what the planter provided, and they "paid" in promissory notes of their labor. Now blacks had choice of what to buy and access to hard currency. The Jews were crucial facilitators. As a sign of their social integration, Jews became a prominent part of the Masonic order in the South and were not excluded because of race/religion as they often were in the North. Catholics often had that distinction.

So here's Dothan, the place Christians had been led to, becoming a promised land for Jews. Hyman Blumberg settled here in 1892 and started in the *schmatta* business. He had seven kids, all of whom worked at the store, soon the largest department store in southeast Alabama— Blumberg and Sons. It was the first store in Dothan to install an escalator. People would come from many miles away just for the ride. But Blumberg's doors closed in 1975, about the same time Sam Walton was making his move across the South with his on-the-outskirts-of-town, price-obsessed, no-escalator Walmarts. In truth, however, Penney's and Sears had already done most of the heavy demolition of the downtown stores.

Dothan was typical of what happened after the Second World War. As downtown businesses struggled, many young Jews moved out. They wouldn't stay. Going out of business was for real and not a marketing gimmick. You can see the results everywhere along U.S. 84. Jewish cemeteries with no upkeep, synagogues in disarray (the most tragic in Natchez), and those downtown husks of once-thriving department stores. That's not because there are no Jews in the South; more Jews are living in the South than ever—about 386,000 at last count in 2001 (according to Stuart Rockoff, historian at the Goldring/Woldenberg Institute of Southern Jewish Life in Jackson, Mississippi). They are just not in small-town Dixie.

In Alabama, for instance, young Jews left towns like Dothan in favor of cities like Birmingham (5,300 Jews), Montgomery (1,200), Mobile

(1,100), and Huntsville (750). Still, only about 9,000 Jews live in the entire state, down from about 12,000 in the 1930s. The real trans-South migration has been to the New South: Atlanta, New Orleans, Charlotte, and the large cities of Florida.

Larry Blumberg, a grandson of Hyman, is chairman of the Blumberg Family Relocation Fund, which is offering Jewish families as much as fifty thousand dollars to relocate to Dothan. The fund put advertisements in Jewish newspapers across the Northeast promising that if you get involved at Temple Emanu-El and stay put in Dothan at least five years, you won't have to repay the money. About twenty Jewish families have sought information about Dothan. No takers.

Like the Jews, Southeastern Xtreme Wrestling has also had trouble keeping its young talent in place. When I tried to contact them back in the fall of 2008, they had gone chapter 11. I saw their old display ads (*Beware of Dog Heavyweight Title Match*) still in various store windows (my favorite being a store called Dirt Cheap, a chain only in Alabama, Mississippi, and Louisiana). What I didn't know was that in February 2009 they rose phoenix-like, or perhaps better, Hulk Hogan–like, to re-enter the fray. Longtime Dothan promoter Will Pritchard came off the mat to give it another try. He's rented an old flea market building—no heat, no air-conditioning—and expects to make ends meet by charging eight hundred dollars to train youngsters in the craft. And maybe put on some exhibitions. He may have better luck finding recruits than Larry Blumberg, but when I drove by: nothing happening.

Too bad, because I was going to ask him how he chose not the victors, but the fall guys. Who needed to get pummeled? If the pantomime of wrestling acts out the anxieties of the young audience, was there ever a carpetbagger type playing the heavy? I knew from watching the national version that the villains are our enemies du jour like al-Qaeda terrorists or any kind of sexual deviant. When I was a kid, the bad guys were mad Russians and wily Japanese. But that was the national, televised version. Did the regional high-school-gym-on-Saturday-night version ever venture into the past to address ancient squabbles? Was there ever a Yankee carpetbagger putting the submission hold on some innocent good ol' boy? I never found out.

Memorializing Villains

Dixie had other villains. We saw this a few miles up the road in a town appropriately called Enterprise. Back at the beginning of the twentieth century, cotton was still king. But traveling along El Camino from Mexico came the boll weevil. In the words of that folk song made famous by Brook Benton, that "little black bug" was "just lookin' for a home."

Boll weevil found one of his many homes in Enterprise. By 1918, farmers were losing whole fields to the beetle in just a few days. An enterprising entrepreneur named H. M. Sessions saw this as an opportunity to convert the area to peanut farming. He saw right. To celebrate this "sweet use of adversity," a local businessman came up with the idea to build a monument to the weevil.

The thirteen-foot statue is right there in the middle of town at the intersection of College and Main streets—a woman wearing a flowing gown, arms stretched above her head, clutching the little critter, a delicate fountain squirting below. Alas, the statue has been defaced a number of times. So what you see today as you stop your car stock still in the middle of town is a replica erected in 1998. The original is safe over at the Depot Museum. Locals seem to have adapted to the perpetual roadblock as if it were just another weevil. Here was the only statue of a human we saw in the South that was not somehow connected to the Civil War. Who says the Dixie doesn't appreciate irony?

I wasn't sure what to make of this memorial other than that the threat to land is more intensely felt here than anywhere else in the United States. In much of the country the concern is with money, with possessions, with what anthropologists call "demonstration goods." People in Manhattan and LA will even squabble over swanky area codes or zip codes, let alone baby carriages and parking spaces. Perhaps with no manufacturing history and no fortunes built on marketing, the South was more medieval in its celebration of land. Being on the same land for generations counted for something. It becomes like blood ancestry. And so taking someone's land away, which is what the carpetbagger and the boll weevil did, made them both images of evil and deserving of some retributive celebration, albeit with varying degrees of playfulness.

Monument in Enterprise, Alabama. The citation reads, "In Profound Appreciation of the Boll Weevil and what it has done as the Herald of Prosperity." That funding came from peanut farmers goes without saying.

Photo by author

The Marketing of Gee's Bend

As I had noticed earlier in Georgia, Dixie is not much interested in the visual arts. Seeing this downtown statue was a hoot. It was fun to look at. We would go for days seeing nothing that was created just for the joy of sensing it. Maybe it's because there were no large towns to support an art museum; maybe it's because there was no time for decorative crafts; maybe it's because there was no history of making things for the simple pleasures of holding them and talking about them. Maybe it's because they had no isolating winter where you go into the wood shop or sit for hours knitting. There were plenty of museums, but they held mostly old farm machinery, footballs, and school yearbooks.

Bob Cohan and his magnificent trailer (it looks like a men's club inside, all decked out in dark wainscoting) finally caught up to us north of Monroeville, Alabama. Bob is a retired pediatric allergist from Pensacola and a serious student of Jews in the South. But he is also fascinated by an extraordinary enclave of African Americans who became a sociological wonder back in the 1930s. They lived just north of U.S. 84 in a crook in the Alabama River called Gee's Bend. In some respects they are like Jews in the European pogroms because they developed an adaptive culture that allowed them to be both visible and invisible to the dominant culture. Bob assured me Gee's Bend was worth a look for any student of the Deep South, even if it meant a side trip from the sacred U.S. 84.

So we scooted north through Monroeville, the literary capital of Alabama, home to Truman Capote and Harper Lee, stopping only long enough to tour the downtown museum cum shrine. The curators have done an admirable job of assimilating two homegrown critics without foregrounding the criticism, and without mentioning some of Mr. Capote's decidedly unsouthernly ways. They even restored the upstairs courtroom of the old town hall to look just like the scene from To Kill a Mockingbird. It should. The movie's set directors were nominated for an Oscar for best mise-en-scène. They copied the original courtroom, inch by inch. And then the museum restored Monroe's aging courtroom to look just like the Hollywood copy. Modern French critics would have a field day with this. No matter, the spirit of Gregory Peck hung heavy in the air. Downstairs, the movie was running in an endless loop.

We were off to follow the spirit of another movie star, Jane Fonda, and this time to look at some real decorative art. This takes some explanation. Back in the Depression, a colony of forsaken blacks were left penned in by a turn in the Alabama River. They were caught in a geographical cul de sac. For the most part, they were descendants of freed slaves who had taken the name of their onetime owner, Mark Pettway.

For years the black Pettways were left high and dry, unable to cross over the river to the nearest town, Camden, because the whites refused to supply a dependable ferry. The ferry ran only to meet demand, and demand was judged from the Camden side by the whites. So the Pettways often had to take the long way round the oxbow to do shopping or to get medical care. They were desperately poor, but they owned much of their own land and learned how to make do. When the WPA writers came through to write the Alabama guide, they completely passed them by. But others visited during the Depression, most notably the photographer Arthur Rothstein and then, in the 1940s, folklorist Robert Sonkin.

The Pettways were developing a parallel culture. They would pick up and discard language, food, habits, fabric, from the whites across the river. No one paid them much mind. One thing that everyone from FDR's Resettlement Administration on noticed, however, was that the women were gathering together to sew patchwork quilts. These quilts were done in brilliant colors using arresting patterns. If one of their shacks had an interesting pattern on the ceiling, they would sew a quilt to imitate it. The quilts were hanging everywhere, almost like flags.

Gee's Bend quilts commemorated in the 2006 "American Treasures" stamp series, U.S. Postal Service

Photo by Mary Twitchell

More intriguing still, the quilts were being passed around so that one quilter could elaborate on some aspect of the imagery in a different quilt, essentially making personal comments in a shared conversation. The concept of single and stable authorship didn't exist. The quilts had a double utility: they provided warmth against the winter cold, but they also carried a memory of community history.

Not much happened in Gee's Bend until the 1960s, when the civil rights movement activated the inhabitants to take the ferry over to Camden to vote. Martin Luther King Jr. even paid them a visit to encourage them to make the trip to the polls. And that predictably caused the local whites to radically curtail the ferry service. From 1962 until 2006, there was essentially no scheduled service, especially during election times.

Like the quilts, Gee's Bend did not go entirely unnoticed. Calvin Trillin did a *New Yorker* piece on the quilting bees in the late 1960s. As photography gained recognition as an art form in the 1970s, the Rothstein black-and-white photos of the quilts became collectors' items. And then, in 1999, came J. R. Moehringer's dreamy piece on Gee's Bend in the *Los Angeles Times*, called "Crossing Over." It won a Pulitzer Prize. This article had everything: oppressed blacks, Bull Connor–type lawmen, voting intimidation, a ferry that didn't run, and again those imaginative, storytelling quilts.

Only one more stitch in the fabric, and that came in 2002. Thanks to the resurgence of interest in folk art and the sensitivity to race issues in art history, an exhibition of the Pettway handiwork was held in the Museum of Fine Arts, Houston. A success, the show then moved to the Whitney Museum in New York City, and from there to an almost continual tour of big-city museums. What had been a way to cover cracks in the sharecropper cabins now became a way to cover alabaster walls in exhibition halls.

And from the museum's point of view, this was a real moneymaker. Not only were the artists women, so too were most of the crowds. And so too most of the shoppers in the museum store. The quilts became blockbuster art and an aftermarket bonanza in museum trinkets. Proof? In August 2006, the United States Postal Service released a sheet of ten commemorative stamps bearing images of Gee's Bend quilts. Even the stamps sold out.

And now the story becomes especially interesting for students of Deep Dixie because all the pieces of the mythic South are in place. We have a powerful narrative fraught with the stereotypes of race relations; we have a dispossessed group—black women—who are exaggerations of gender inequities elsewhere; and we have a substance that cannot be questioned, namely, the stuff of art. If these quilts were not art, then what were they doing on those museum walls and why were reproductions being sold in museum shops?

And that brings us to Jane Fonda. Jane Fonda has a daughter by Roger Vadim named Vanessa. For a while, Vanessa was married to Mark Arnett. Mark's dad, William, is an Atlanta art dealer who, more than anyone, was responsible for marketing the quilts as works of art. And not without a little self-dealing. In the 1950s and 1960s, he bought about a hundred of them for a pittance. Many of the touring quilts were his. Like many savvy collectors, he would lend quilts to museums, have their value increase, and then take them to his gallery and sell them. Nothing new here. Pop Art collectors were doing this all the time with oil paintings. In addition, he did what many collectors did. He published a hefty coffee-table book extolling the artistic nature of his objects. The objects were noticed, as was he himself.

This is the context in which Ms. Vadim made a documentary called *The Quiltmakers of Gee's Bend* that has been shown on PBS stations around the country. The program was part of the publicity machine that was generating the market value for the quilts. When you go to Gee's Bend and enter the little converted schoolhouse that is the home of the quilters at work, you will see this show played in an endless loop on a TV monitor. It is the standard PBS puff piece, complete with heroic music and intense talking faces from various museums assuring you that what you are seeing here is in a direct line from Matisse and Klee—the unconscious influence of color and form.

Don't believe it? Here's a bit from the transcript:

01:13:41:12: Sitting interview with David Gordon [director, Milwaukee Art Museum].

GORDON: If you had asked this woman, these women "Are you artists?" until recently, they would have said, "No. We are just doing this be-

85

cause it comes naturally." So our definitions of artists and outsider artists are all thrown into question.

01:13:57:11: Sitting interview with Alvia Wardlaw [curator, Museum of Fine Art, Houston].

WARDLAW: These quilts are important as contemporary art for several reasons. Um, the first being that they represent a tradition that has been passed on for a number of generations in a very small area in America: Gee's Bend, Alabama. The quilts reflect the history of that area and of this country in their making and it asks all of us about genius, you know, and where does it reside?

01:40:50:19: Nonie Gadsden [associate curator of decorative arts, Milwaukee] speaking to a group.

GADSEN: There's two reasons why this show is so important. One is the art. It's the quilts. Seeing the composition, the bold patterns, the asymmetry. These quilts are fantastic works of art. What you're seeing is things that came out of the women's mind. They had no influences. A lot of people make connections with these works, and works of modern contemporary art. They didn't know Barnett Newman's work. They didn't know Joseph Alber's work. These designs came out of their own heads. And I want to make sure that we all know and give them that agency. These are the artists who created this work. They are not copying anybody else. This came out of their heart and this is what they created. Second, it's Gee's Bend. The story of Gee's Bend and the history of Gee's Bend. (www.aptv.org/AS/GeesBend/GeesAssets/geesscriptrevised.pdf)

These pages are not the place to discuss how much modern art is created, but suffice it to say that for some critics (myself included), art is whatever these art curators say it is. In other words, if you see it often enough inside a museum, bingo! it's art. Likewise, literature is what's inside anthologies. We may like to think that we know it when we see it, but if art history tells us anything, it tells us that is nonsense. Unlike Potter Stewart's definition of pornography, the appreciation of art is learned, not instinctive. And we learn it by seeing it in a particular place and hearing a particular person talk about it in special language.

It's in this context that Jane Fonda plays an important role. As these images are spinning past us, music swells, and the filmmaker's mother appears on camera:

01:02:06:02: Sitting interview with Jane Fonda.

FONDA: I fell in love with the art. It's all left over things that have been discarded by others the way they, the artists, have been discarded by society. And they take these discarded pieces and give them new and transcendent life. . . . The, the, the art is so full of love and patriotism and hope, is very moving, you know. . . . The rest of us can get cynical and angry. These people of all people should be, and they're not. (www.aptv.org/as/GeesBend/GeesAssets/geesscriptrevised.pdf)

What struck me most as we were at the little schoolhouse with the sign "Gee's Bend Quilters" over the door was how little quilting was going on. This place was all about *selling*, not sewing. Quilts were stacked up for sale in the corners. On one side of the building was an empty room lined with black-and-white art photos of Gee's Bend folk. And on the other side, the side with the stacked quilts, were three square-faced women, one darning and the other two sitting in front of a gas heater. One of them had a Tommy Hilfiger toque on. In the background was the looping television show with those curators and Jane Fonda talking about the quilts as art. It was hard not to feel the urge to buy something. If you were sitting in Picasso's studio in the 1930s, and you knew what you know now, wouldn't you buy a painting?

Then you look at the quilts. They are piled up like shirts in a Ralph Lauren store with prices to match: $2,500 to $4,000. Each has a little tag with the quilter's name. We are told that the ones in the museum were selling for $80,000, and that's if we were lucky enough to buy one. Of course we can't. Mr. Arnett owns most of those, about seven hundred, some of which he bought for as little as forty dollars apiece. No matter, it's time to quit looking and buy.

My pal Bob pulls one out from the pile and says it's too expensive, and one of the ladies looks at the tag and says she knows the quilter and we can negotiate. Maybe that's what is meant by communal production. Bob has already told her he's from Florida, and she says with a smile, "Buy it now, you know you can afford it." These women have done this before. He buys a small eighteen-inch-square patch for fifty-four dollars.

Meanwhile the woman with the Tommy Hilfiger cap has spotted me for the Yankee tightwad I am, and she says flatly, "You not gonna buy," and points me to the straw bowl of Toblerone bars—the triangular Swiss chocolate bars. Next to it is a cigar box stuffed with dollar bills. "At least buy a candy bar." I freeze. Am I that obvious? And what is *that* brand of chocolate doing here? Clearly, I'm not the first reluctant male led into this retail trap.

As a teacher of English (and a sometimes teacher of advertising), I am interested in how luxury objects are sold because it's really all about concentrated storytelling. All high-end commercial objects aspire to the condition of art. That's why the objects at Louis Vuitton or Gucci stores are heroically lit as if they were in a museum. Often they have a little tag on them explaining provenance, just like paintings. That's why the top-end stores are often in the same neighborhoods as museums. That's why the narrative that travels with the object is so important: why the polo pony is on the shirt chest not just on the label, why LV initials are splashed across luggage. It's why the painter's signature is so important to see; why we know the names of designers like Tom Ford, Karl Lagerfeld, Miuccia Prada, or Ralph Lauren.

Look at the ads in *Vanity Fair* or the *New Yorker* or the first few pages of the Sunday *New York Times* and you'll understand that luxury hype works best when the underlying object is simple. That's why handbags, shoes, T-shirts, scarves, eyeglasses, watches, and the like can get goosed-up into the land of de luxe. Think bottled water. The taste is not in the water, it's in the advertising—in the story.

Now don't get me wrong. The original quilts, the ones made in the 1930s, are really extraordinary. But they have been pretty well culled out. What I was seeing at Gee's Bend Quilters Inc. was what even Bloomingdale's had passed by. What is currently being produced seems to me shallow and cookie-cut. And I wasn't the only one perplexed. I found out later that there has been a flurry of lawsuits between the lawyers for the quilters and the Arnetts. William Arnett was the subject of a *60 Minutes* investigation in the 1990s that questioned his dealings with folk artists. He was also the focus of a nonfiction novel called *The Last Folk Hero: A True Story of Race and Art, Power and Profit.* Say what you want, however, the Arnetts know how to generate narrative value for the quilts—one of their self-published books on the quilts is titled *Souls Grow Deep.* Nothing tops that!

The future business plan for Gee's Bend Corp. seems to be to use the startling imagery of the original quilts on other objects—machine-made, mass-produced objects—in what's called *brand extension.* So Kathy Ireland World Marketing, a kind of Martha Stewart for decorators, uses the imagery on tablecloths, patterned ties, scarves, coffee mugs, and refrigerator magnets. Ireland, a former supermodel and Southern California celebrity mom, says there will be no toilet seats, shower curtains, or mouse pads on her watch. Her major outlets are Costco and Kmart.

She's not alone. Anthropologie, the upscale mall store, licensed a copy of an early Gee's Bend quilt, makes it on a mechanical loom in Asia, and sells it for $298. And the Classic Rug Collection has some twenty-three replicas complete with faded colors, frays, and stains for under $200. It's almost like buying jeans. In fact, that's precisely what the quilts are becoming.

No wonder the women are sitting there. They know where the money is. It's not in making the objects; it's in telling the story to make the objects valuable. And just their presence, complete in the Hilfiger toque with the television running in the background, does exactly that. Supposedly the licensing arrangements have netted the community more than a million dollars in trust. Looking around Gee's Bend, I didn't see where that money was going. But when I looked at the lawsuits, I noticed many of the Pettways are living in Mobile.

I must say I felt ambivalent. These descendants of the Pettways, a family that used the techniques of collage and adaptation to do what the Ruskinites could not do, namely, form an almost utopian community based on the dignity of work, are now almost paste-ups of their grandmothers.

I didn't buy the Yuppie chocolate. Perhaps I should have. After all, it's not their fault that sitting around is what they do. They have moved into celebrity culture, a make-believe simulation of the ancient Gee's Bend.

In a sense they have exchanged their oxbow separation for a more modern kind of separation: they now play the role of quilter without having to do the stitching. They have become brand stewards in the museum-industrial complex. As we drove back down to U.S. 84, I couldn't help but wonder if here in this little cul de sac of southern culture, the myth of the happy darkie (Huck Finn's Jim, Aunt Jemima, Clemence in *The Grandissimes*, Uncle Jack, Sam in *Uncle Tom's Cabin*) was being played out to the satisfaction of both North and South.

On the Road Again

Back on U.S. 84 again we headed through Grove Hill, Alabama, stopping at Gene & Ellen's Drive-In, which has burgers so good that truckers simply park their rigs in the middle of the downtown street to eat there. And while there we walked over to the sweet Clarke County Historical Museum. I know *sweet* is not a usual term for museum judging, but this one is. This kind of collection is something we encountered in a number of southern towns. We saw one in Blakely, Georgia, the Early County Museum, where we were shown around by a grandfatherly fellow who told us how awful the Yankees had been during Reconstruction. These museums are put together by loving people, people who, near the end of their lives, want to share the things they treasured. Of course, by this time the objects have little market value. But you know that when the objects (stuff from the war, tools, clothing, yearbooks, a few toys . . .) came into their lives, they were precious. But again, what I found interesting was that these were not decorative items but things obtained along the way as part of getting through life. They were mostly rude necessities, not whimsical ornaments.

Moving through this kind of museum is rather like going to see your ancient granny. When you get to the door to leave, she begs you to please take this knickknack, and you look at it and you don't really want it, but you look at granny and you know it's important to her. So you do. It's not the object that carries the value; it's that it has such value to her. I haven't seen this kind of museum in New England. I think it might be laughed at, not appreciated for the gift it is. It made me realize once again that southern life had more in common with the frontier life of North Dakota than with the confected romances of Natchez.

In the Clarke County Historical Museum is a memorial to the men who died for their country in the First World War. On one side of a granite slab (it looks like a gravestone) are the names of the deceased whites. On the other side are the names of the deceased blacks. The two sides have about the same number of names. The memorial once stood in the center of town and was unearthed for obvious reasons. A new monument with all the names bunched together was put in its place. The old monument went to the museum. I wasn't sure what to make of this. On one hand, I'm sure the separation of names was a reflex, and on the other, I wondered about how such a reflex could escape the recognition that dying for your country pretty much trumps the neatness of segregation. Anyway, I thought it important that the curators understood that whatever it meant, it was important enough to be saved in a museum.

Why was it that so many of the nostalgic creations of the Old South—Yardell (the lawn jockey), Aunt Jemima, "Way Down upon the Swanee River," cake walking, Al Jolson in blackface, pickaninny dolls, Uncle Ben, *Gone with the Wind*, Little Black Sambo—appear between the world wars. Today they are considered caricatures, but they certainly weren't back in the early twentieth century.

Could it be that the same tensions that caused the town fathers of Grove Hill to reengrave the slab account for this paradox? The desire to infantalize the black, to make him/her into a one-dimensional character, to put their names on the *other* side of the tablet, only works when you can delude yourself into thinking your life is somehow different from theirs. They are the *other*. But once they are dying for you—in those unmarked graves of Flanders Fields—the myth falls apart. You may try to reenslave them with Jim Crow laws, but you still have to cope with the deep realization that a black person just died for your country and that this death is every bit as real as the death of your loved one. Death, to rewrite Dr. Johnson, does indeed "concentrate the mind." It is the great equalizer. It does not discriminate. Seeing this mixed-up monument made me realize that maybe the First World War had to come before Reconstruction.

Bladon Springs

Our little caravan pulled into Bladon Springs State Park before twilight, and we made camp. By this time—we had been on the X axis for weeks—we were a well-oiled team, each with our little chores. I did the rig leveling, plugged in the water, electric, and sewer. Mary did everything else. The southern state parks, at least the ones we stayed in from Georgia to Louisiana, are uniformly clean and inviting. Often they are on a picturesque lake. In this case, the park was built around a couple of ancient springs. The springs were in a little hollow and drizzled sulphuric water.

Back in its heyday before the Civil War, this smelly water was sought for its curative properties, and a Greek revival hotel was built for the ailing pilgrims. This hotel was cavernous, possibly the largest wooden building in the state, and featured a ballroom, a bowling alley, a billiard room, and even a skating rink. I was glad to see it had had a bar in the basement level, a sign of more sensible times. Bladon Springs became known as the "Saratoga of the South." It stayed open until the end of the century, when the jig was up for smelly mineral water. Later, in a sign of what transpired all over the Deep South, the hotel was used by loggers who had come in to harvest the yellow pine. The hotel burned in the late 1930s. Not much remains other than a few bricks from the pilings—even the WPA writers passed it by.

In fact, today Bladon Springs is a melancholy spot. We were the only ones staying the night and it was a little scary, what with the ruins and the drizzling sulfuric springs. No park ranger came by to collect our fees and tuck us in. I had read of a robbery in an RV park on the Winnebago View Web site, and now the confines of our little sardine can seemed more a trap than a recreational vehicle. So after an uneasy night I was happy to see the next morning bright and clear. We said good-bye to Bob, who was heading back to Pensacola, and prepared to pack up.

That's how we met Willie Campbell. He was the ranger. I was inside the rig doing something, and I could hear Mary outside talking with him. The two of them were not moving, just standing, talking. After a while I decided to join them. Maybe I was a little anxious, I don't remember. Willie is a black man and in his dark brown park uniform he seemed all of the same hue.

Willie must be my age—mid-sixties—and he was just chatting. Bob had left without paying, and we were explaining what had happened. We thought there was no ranger. One subject led to another, and soon we were talking about our trip. We chatted about where we were going, what had happened to my family in the 1870s, and what I expected to see. I found that when I told someone I was trying to understand the Deep South by driving across U.S. 84, they either understood it or not. Willie said he understood. He said to watch out when we got to Louisiana. The first thing a southerner thinks about when a Yankee comes to call is that the Yankee is going to take his land.

I told him about the Colfax massacre, and he said he'd never heard of it. But he wasn't surprised. I told him about the slaughter of my kinfolk, and he said he never heard of such a thing. Whites don't kill whites like that unless blacks are involved. He remembered hearing about lynchings when he was a kid. He said if a black boy was seen in the company of a white girl, the black kid would have to go away. As simple as that. A friend of his was observed in a field with a white girl, and he never saw his friend again. If a black man had a white friend who would vouch for him, that might help. Otherwise, stay apart.

I think the best way to explain what happened that morning is to tell you that Willie's voice is just like Denzel Washington's. Now I know this sounds stagey, but I often have trouble understanding black speech (I'm also a little deaf), and Willie was clear as the proverbial bell. That is, once I got over some of the turns of phrase.

The best analogy I can think of was that our conversation was like those I used to have as a teenager on the Greyhound bus. There was no point being coy, you were getting off in a few hours, so what the hell. I confessed my lack of understanding of the South—why for instance things took so long to get done, and, now that a black man was in the White House, why couldn't we get this racial stuff behind us. He smiled. He said it wasn't going to happen.

In fact, he said that he used to get together in the morning before work with men friends up the road at a junction of U.S. 84 and 17 in a little town called Silas. The men were both white and black. There was an Exxon station on one side and a quick stop of some kind on the other.

Both stations had small coffee tables. On the morning after the election of Obama, the races separated.

I didn't take that as much more than a temporary recalibration of forces, but then he started telling stories of what life was like as a black man in Alabama. Although he had come from these parts, he had gone to Mobile, where he had worked his way up to becoming a plant supervisor for Scott Paper. He worked in a huge paper-making plant, in charge of some aspect of running the machinery. He had to delegate tasks for workers and he tried to be fair, but he knew the whites were always thinking of him first as a black man. A "nigger boss," he said, is hard for whites.

So I asked him when did he first know this about whites, and he said that as a child, maybe ten years old, a relative had died, and his mother had asked him to go over to the rich white woman's house to ask her to make a phone call for them. This woman was the only one in the neighborhood with a phone, and Willie's mom needed to notify the kin. So he went up to the woman's house and knocked on the door. She came to the door. He told her that his mother would like the woman to call "Mr. Sam" to tell him his sister had died. The woman seemed to understand and was willing to do the favor. Willie turned to walk away. After she moved back into the house, she "whirled back" and called to him, "Nigger, come back here." Willie came back to the door. She glowered. "Don't let me ever hear you call a nigger *Mister* again."

What I thought was even more powerful is that as he's telling me this he's not really criticizing the woman. In fact, he says it's in her *raisin'*. I look dubious, and he says that he doesn't believe she was mean—she was just *raised mean*. She's still living, and her young granddaughter calls Willie *Mister*. But he knows, he says, what's in the raising.

Years ago his own son was shot and killed. Willie says that his son was just the wrong person at the wrong place, but he says that while the act was horrendous, he does not hate the killer. He did go up to the parole board to say that he doesn't want the killer to be free, but that's not because of the person but because of the act. He can forgive the person.

Now I'm not ready for this kind of Christianity. I've only encountered it a few times in my life. Genuine forgiveness is never so rare, I've found, as among Christians professing compassion. Willie told me that he thinks prejudice is the devil, that when you are cruel without cause it's literally the devil inside you.

One of the reasons why there are so few people in Bladon Park is that the local whites don't want to use it because Willie is black. They don't think a black man should be in charge, even if he's qualified. They don't even want the state park signs to be posted along U.S. 84. That's okay with Willie; it means less work. He smiles an impish smile.

Willie is the only black ranger in the Alabama park system. When they have their yearly meetings, he is clearly the odd man out, and, as he says, he has to be careful where he sits. But he says that his boss's wife always gives him a big welcoming hug so that makes it easier. He says that public display "makes everyone's eyes buckle." When he talks about the racial animosity he never despairs, but he is clearly not optimistic.

In fact, Willie likes watching Sean Hannity on Fox News because it gives him an understanding. He says he won't use words like *redneck* or *cracker* or something that sounds like "poojer," which I had never heard of. What good do they do? he asked.

When he was at Scott Paper, there was always trouble with the high-speed paper-cutting machinery. One day a white worker suggested that they could "nigger rig" a bit of broken equipment. The underling caught himself and said they could "Polish rig" the equipment, which of course made no sense. Willie said he understood what had happened. Later the man came up to him to apologize. The man himself was French and had married a Creole woman, and he knew what it meant to be slurred. It was clear that this apology was a powerful experience to Willie. It doesn't happen often.

Willie said he plans to retire in December. He says some of the locals will be happy to get their park back. Maybe they'll start using it again. I understand why the boss's wife hugged him. When we parted, Mary did too. I realized I was sensing something I had not appreciated in Georgia. If the whites had these elaborate codes of besmirched honor, blacks had this dignity of passive endurance. Both were obviously connected to the institution of slavery but even more so to the wrenching contortions of Reconstruction. Willie had been sold out by the North and, in a weird sense, so too had the attackers of my great-grandfather. What an irony that genuine betrayal resulted in resigned compassion while prolonged disgrace produced self-righteous outrage and bloody violence. Maybe both responses were, in the lingo of pop psychology, inappropriate. Maybe things were now changing. A black man was president. Certainly something had moved along the Y axis, whether Willie agreed or not.

④

Mississippi, the Most Southern Place on Earth

> We can't boast of our ancestors because, when we get started talking about
> our families, out jumps the ghost of a pirate or a cousin of color.
> —SAM DABNEY, FROM JAMES STREET'S *Tap Roots*, 1943

Crossing over into Mississippi we noticed two things: first, this state is getting the jump on its neighbors by starting to build Interstate 14 along the side of U.S. 84. In places the large blue background exit signs announcing lodging, gas, and fast food are already up. Someone needs to tell them the other states are not cooperating. And, second, we noticed that the best-looking buildings in Mississippi are the banks. They seem to be everywhere, clean and neat with big pillars. Maybe Willie Sutton was right; that's where the money is. It doesn't seem to be anywhere else. There's a famous quote that there are more writers in Mississippi than people who can read, and I couldn't help churlishly wondering if there are more banks in Mississippi than there are businesses with money. Or maybe these are the banks not doing the credit default swaps.

The Free State of Jones

The chunk of east-central Mississippi you enter on U.S. 84 has a unique history. It was settled by the same cantankerous Scotch-Irish who moved west from the Carolinas, Virginia, and Georgia. They were Celts—think *Braveheart.* The land never was very productive, and timbering hadn't yet begun. These settlers didn't have slaves. They did have religion, however. Over to the west, in the Mississippi Delta, there was cotton aplenty. And slaves to produce it. But here in the rolling hills, it was really one-mule-a-family farming. So when the wealthier parts of the South wanted war, this area wanted none of it. Why should they?

And so the myth of the rebellious Jones County (named for John Paul Jones) began. Supposedly when the question of secession from the Union came up, the Jones County people voted it down. They said, no thanks, we have no interest in fighting so that you can keep your slaves. They instructed their delegate to the secession convention in Jackson to vote no. But when he arrived in the big city, he was caught up in the furor and voted with the Rebels. His angry neighbors back home hanged him in effigy.

Reluctantly, Jones County prepared for war. They made their reluctance public, and the Confederate cavalry, whose initial job was to find food and supplies for the army, descended on them. The Rebels raided their farms, taking food and livestock that these people could ill afford to lose. One of those farmers was taciturn Newt Knight, and he was an early conscientious objector. He refused to fight for a cause he did not believe in, and when he was drafted, he served not as a combatant but as a hospital orderly.

But he didn't serve for long. Once he learned of the infamous "Twenty Negro Law" (if a man owned twenty or more slaves, he could avoid military service) and once he had been traumatized by battle (the bloody fight at Corinth), Newt became an active objector. This fight was becoming "a rich man's war and a poor man's fight." He deserted and returned home to Jones County.

He didn't come home alone. There were plenty of other deserters from this part of Mississippi. About a hundred of them holed up right along U.S. 84 in a place called Leaf River Swamp, near the present town of Soso. As with so much of the South, this swampland would be drained after the war to get to timber. But in the 1850s it was sopping wet. The deserters would commute from the boggy bivouac, called Devil's Den, to their farms, work the land, hunt and fish, and, when pursued, retreat into the muck.

What became known as the Newt Knight Company and the Free State of Jones was an embarrassment, to say nothing of the drain on the war effort, and so the Confederate headquarters in Jackson decided to put an end to Newt. They sent a Major Amos McLemore, a native of Jones County and a man who supposedly knew the swamps, to take him out. He came close, but Newt was too savvy, surprising McLemore and shooting him point-blank in the head. From then on, Newt was left alone. He seems to have spent a quiet retirement, working his land and, as we will see, populating his swamp families, one black, one white. He lived until 1922.

It's a great sidebar story and of course had many additions (most obviously the numbers; in some versions Newt leads hundreds of commandos). Even Ken Burns gives him a tip of the hat in his Civil War documentary. And Newt's been the subject of a number of books, most recently Sally Jenkins and John Stauffer's *The State of Jones* (2009). Clearly, as time went on, many versions of the story came from the North because it shows that the South was not united into a true Confederacy. In some of these renditions, Newt is taking his orders from Yankee generals after the victory in Vicksburg.

But leave it to Hollywood to amp up this myth with its adaptation of a book called *Tap Roots*, by James Street. In 1948, Newt's adventures were made into a movie of the same name in which Ward Bond plays the reluctant hero (called Hoab Dabney, as in the book), who darts in and out of the swamp blowing things up in the then-new Technicolor. Somehow in this movie Mississippi has become quite hilly. Hoab/Newt has a daughter, the swarthily made-up Susan Hayward. Did the moviemakers know something they weren't telling about this daughter? Not much is made of this (as it was, say, in Yvonne De Carlo's role in *Band of Angels*), but she seems to be of mixed race.

Now fast-forward to real life. In the same year the movie was released, one of Newt's great-grandchildren, Davis Knight, got arrested. Davis had come back from World War II to settle down to a quiet life of farming near the old family homestead in Soso. He married a blue-eyed girl. The police said he was a Negro. Seems that a relative, still upset about ancient family transgressions during the Civil War, figured out that Davis's bloodline went back to Newt's dalliance with Rachel, a black woman. She was an escaped slave living in that swamp.

But that's not what is shocking. This is: on June 21, 1948, a court in Ellisville convicted Newt's great-grandson of miscegenation, sentencing him to five years in jail. In November of the next year, the Mississippi Supreme Court overturned this verdict on equally amazing grounds. It held that it had not been proven that Rachel was "of full African ancestry." Instead of dealing with the nonsense of miscegenation, the court preferred to think Rachel might be a Creole or an Indian. Davis was legally deemed a *white Negro*. The most compelling aspect of the myth of the white Negro is that the South is nothing but white Negroes, or, if you prefer, Negroid whites. As any honest southerner will tell you, if a drop of black blood will make you Negroid, then the entire Old White South was only old and south.

As we know, miscegenation was commonplace in the South, so much so that slaveholders often took special care of their mixed-blood offspring. The dynamics of this must have been bewildering. For instance, Newt's white wife left him in a jealous rage, and his twin families squabbled for a generation but then intermingled without regard for blood links. Still more bewildering is the occasional use of the law as bulwark *forbidding* the truth. Punishing the son for the putative sins of the father is ridiculous enough, but then whimsically pretending to be like Captain Renault in Casablanca—"Shocked. Just Shocked"—is turning the world upside down. I realized I was seeing another example of the granite memorial with the names written on opposite sides. I was beginning to understand what Willie Campbell had told me: it's not easy being a dedicated racist. You have to give up reality. You have to be eternally vigilant. You can't let the irregularities of truth through. Perhaps that's why when Obama wins, the groups separate, not unite. Maybe that partially explains why my kin were killed.

Squirrel Dogs along U.S. 84

Back in the summer when I had been planning my Dixieland tour, I knew I was going to run aground in mid-Mississippi. Just look at any roadmap and you'll see the problem. There's a big gap to the east of Laurel and an even bigger gap to the west. I knew part of the far western gap was the vast Mississippi Delta, but I wasn't sure about the open stretch from Laurel to Brookhaven. Even the WPA scribes who had been able to find objects of interest in the dreariest places drew a blank. In their tour no. 11 from Waynesboro to Natchez on U.S. 84 they couldn't find much to do other than to note some churches, talk about Newt, and mention some bank robberies. I guess even then the banks had all the money.

So what I did was to search LexisNexis for "Route 84 Mississippi." Here's what appeared. The major cultural importance of U.S. 84 in these parts is that the roadway divides the hunting seasons in Mississippi. North of the road is one season for deer, turkey, rabbit, squirrel, hogs, and bear, and south of the road is another season. The same is true for birds like quail, dove, and partridge. Not so for other waterfowl. They pay U.S. 84 no mind.

So I e-mailed Bobby Cleveland, the outdoor editor of the *Jackson Clarion-Ledger*, to ask if there was a sportsman along this demarcation line who could explain what men do in all these various hunting seasons. Do they suffer from panic disorder about when/what/where they're hunting? Clearly the answer to the old canard of why did the chicken cross the road, especially if the road is U.S. 84, is to get into a safer season.

Bobby e-mailed me back a name he said was ideal, a man who was something of a hero in these parts, Jeffrey Woods. And what made Jeffrey special was that he was one of the premier squirrel hunters in the country, and he was breeding a champion squirrel dog at his Etehoma Creek kennel. He was a legitimate cultural heir of Newt. He even lived in the wonderfully named town of Soso.

Jeffrey's kennel is just northwest of Laurel on a ridge overlooking the swamps that protected Newt. When the swamps were dried out, expansive stands of yellow pine grew in and around the older hardwood nut trees (oak, beechnut, hickory). Squirrels love to gambol about in these woods. This is squirrel Valhalla; you name the subspecies, they are here. Fox squirrels, eastern grays, western grays, tassel-eared, two kinds of flying squirrel (southern and northern), and then the so-called pine squirrels —red and Douglas. You may go to Alaska for salmon, to Paris for fashion, to Taiwan for computer chips, to Bombay for gin, but you go to midstate Mississippi for squirrels.

So I called Jeffrey, told him about my trip, and he said come on by and he'd show me how a country boy can survive. And so I did. In these rolling woods at the end of a meandering road is a magical spot, the Etehoma Creek Kennel. It's a bosky dell with a pine-needle carpet and then a canopy of tall pines, oaks in between. You can hear the dogs from about a quarter mile away, and as you get closer you see them: a big penful of dogs that look like Jack Russells on stilts.

The dogs are called mountain curs or feists, and here's what they do. They lock on to a squirrel in the treetops. Then they essentially point that squirrel until he moves, and then they track him by watching him leap from limb to limb. What makes this doubly interesting is that a squirrel pees when running, just like a rat, and the dogs can track this pee as it floats down from the treetops. So, when the dog is working, his head is bobbing up and down like one of those toy ducks drinking from a glass of water.

It's not an easy job because unlike coon dogs or bloodhounds, who can pick up a scent and then follow it head-down, these bobble-headed dogs have to use their eyes as well as their noses. The squirrels use the air like a footpath. So the dogs have to be trained with special care. To do this, Jeffrey has built a series of conical walkways out of chicken wire and suspended them high off the ground in the kennel. The walkways have little resting platforms. He puts the squirrel on the platform inside the wire mesh and then puts some food way down the walkway on another platform. Sooner or later the hungry squirrel leaves his perch to travel down to the food. When the squirrel starts his trek, the dogs, who live below these walkways, go nuts. They start to follow the squirrel as he moves, then point him as he stops, then follow him again, and again, and again. Essentially, they contract a dreadful case of OCD.

I love Tex Avery cartoons. He made them for MGM in the 1940s. One of my favorite characters is Screwball "Screwy" Squirrel. Screwy is forever being pursued by a dopey dog called Meathead Dog. Screwy is like Bugs Bunny, Woody Woodpecker, and Daffy Duck in that he is (like the pubescent moviegoer) a terrible pest to his elders, but unlike them, he never, never lets up. Bugs, Woody, and Daffy have limits. Screwy is, well, screwy. He'll go on forever.

In one of his most irrepressible escapades, he spends the entire cartoon clobbering Meathead with anything he can find in a trunk labeled "Assorted Swell Stuff to Hit Dog on Head." When he finishes, Meathead remarks, "Gee whiz! He hit me with everything but the kitchen sink!" You know what's coming next. "Well, I don't want to disappoint ya, chum!" squeals Screwy. In the final cartoon in the MGM series, we learn that Screwy is no more. Meathead calmly looks into the camera and observes, "I had a little friend once, but he don't move no more."

It's helpful to keep this cartoon in mind and to remind yourself that a squirrel is just a big rat with a Louis Vuitton tail because these dogs are the revenge of Meathead. They won't quit. And Jeffrey is a cherubic-faced man of about forty who lives knee-deep in these critters. When we meet him, he is wearing a Mississippi tourist T-shirt and a long ponytail. He's leaning against his pickup truck, a truck festooned with decals from dog food companies, his sponsors. I felt I was in a Tennessee hollow and meeting Festus, the ole hunter.

Like all good hunters, Jeffrey has little interest in killing his prey. He kills a lot of squirrels, about 1,200 a year. He'd already done in about 850 by the time we started chatting, and the season was about to end on this side of Route 84. He sells the tails, and the fur is used for fishing lures. He also takes the meat home and boils it up to make a gumbo. Use plenty of cayenne pepper, he suggests. But what he really likes is pitting his mind, and especially his dog, against the squirrel. He wants to get a shot, not take a shot.

And what he really likes is hunting trials where he brings out his dog, prepares the dog to lock on to a particular squirrel ("timber him"), and then "winds" the squirrel as he jumps treetop to treetop, peeing all the time, for a set period of time. Jeffrey and his dogs are national champions. As he is describing the excitement of the chase, his girlfriend, Darlene, drives up. They've been friends since childhood, and she lives nearby. He asks if I want to see his champion dog, and I say yes, and he nods to Darlene and off he goes.

We chat up Darlene, and she's full of smiles. She appreciates Jeffrey's passion. That's one reason she's come back to this area. She misses the people, the sense of being at home, and getting back on *the land*. Jeffrey returns with a black-and-tan feist, and he drops to his knees and scratches the dog's belly. I think the dog's name is Hardwood Bo. My wife asks if she can take a picture, and Jeffrey and Bo immediately assume the dog-photo position, with Jeffrey kneeling and the dog stretching out in the squirrel-pointing position. They've done it before. I look at Darlene. She has a wonderful gap-tooth smile. She knows Jeffrey has more than one passion.

Jeffrey has trouble parting with his dogs, but selling them is his business. A good squirreler can easily sell for five thousand dollars. But sometimes they have to come back for training because the OCD can rub off if the owner is careless and lets the dog dally with the obsession. So some of the dogs are here in the kennel reloading on how to respond to Screwy Squirrel.

Jeffrey also loves hunting with kids. Squirrel hunting is the coming-of-age experience of youngsters in the Deep South. Come October, a father and his son will head off into the woods with a squirrel dog, and the kid will learn not just how to hunt but how to enjoy being outdoors. This tradition is getting lost, and it's more than a tradition; hunting is a family memory. Jeffrey himself remembers how he used to go out in the fall with his dad and brothers. One time he got so tired he fell asleep, and they just left him there and came back to get him hours later. That's okay, at least he was outdoors.

Another time he was crawling in the undergrowth, sneaking up on a turkey, and he got bitten in the shoulder by a water moccasin. He grabbed the snake and held onto it for dear life. When he got to the emergency room, the nurse asked what bit him, and he pulled out the snake from behind his back. She almost fainted. But he had been told by his dad to be sure to bring in the snake so they could tell what bit him. He and Darlene smiled.

I realized that Jeffrey is the southern man we don't know from media-made Dixie. He's the hardworking (his moneymaking job is as a mechanic in a nearby garage, not as a squirreler), caring, passionate man who, like Americans elsewhere, is just trying to get by. He's a good ol' boy, that's for sure. Visit his Web site and look at his hunting pictures and you'll see what I mean (www.etehomacreekkennels.net/photos.html). But he's not spitting tobacco, tossing beer cans, and tending his mullet. He's raising his son, working with his dad and brothers, and traveling around the South teaching kids to do what he loves, hunt. They love it, he says. They have to get "off the asphalt and on to the land."

Jeffrey and Newt Knight live near a little town called Soso. Supposedly the town was named because a stranger asked how things were, and the answer was so-so. But I was struck that Jeffrey and Newt were men of passions and that these passions were for this land, land that I myself considered so-so. We walked all around the town. I still didn't see what was special, but maybe that's exactly what makes it so. In Dixie, it's dangerous to get between a man and his land. I was coming to appreciate that. I'm not sure my great-grandfather did.

High Culture in the Deep South

We decided to spend some more time in mid-Mississippi, not so much to find out anything special (it certainly did seem kind of so-so) as to just see what really was there. Plus there's that big opening gap on the X axis to the west. So I decided I'd attend the two shrines of opposing culture: a Baptist megachurch and a high-culture art museum. Laurel, Mississippi, has both.

The art museum is right downtown. It's spectacular. Once again, it's those Yankees coming down after the war for the cypress and pine who bring along a culture that is a bit contrary, maybe just extraneous. In this case it's some more midwesterners, the Eastman, Gardiner, and Rogers families, who moved in to do what the southerners didn't know how to do. Not cut the timber, but run the railroad lines into the swamps to get the timber. This was happening after the Civil War, as we were finding out, all across the Deep South.

In fact, Yankee railroad mania was sweeping the nation. Recall that at the same time the southern forests were being plundered, the New York and Sacramento railroad barons were laying the transcontinental tracks of the Central and Union Pacific. Making railroads run over difficult terrain was one of the technologies mastered by the North during the war. But here was yet another version of Reconstruction—the de-

struction of southern forests for the construction of northern infrastruc-
ture: bridges, buildings, tunnel supports, roadways, restraining walls,
pilings, all came from these swamps. After the Great Fire, many Chicago
tenements were rebuilt using southern cypress. Not only were they fire-
resistant, they were termite-proof.

And the pillage of this unique resource seems to have been accepted
by the locals in a way that the carpetbaggers were not. For the obvious
reasons. The lumber barons were not mucking around with the social hierarchy, just the natural one. And they weren't even buying the land, just
buying the crop. All around us still were "tree farms." It was like cotton.
Laurel was a mill town, a plantation town; the whirling saw had replaced
the whirling cotton gin. In fact, much of the lumbering was done by
blacks who lived in company housing, eerily reminiscent of double-pen
slave cabins. It seemed ironic that it was the blacks who, after the war,
labored to destroy the very swamps that had earlier been their sanctuary.

In 1921, the scion of one of these Yankee families, Lauren Rogers, died
of appendicitis after graduating from Princeton and before coming back
to run the business. As a memorial, the families set up this art museum
on the site of the home that was being built for him by his father. They
did quite a job. This place looks just like a big-city downtown museum, a
great chunk of Georgian revival in limestone with huge windows and big
columns out front. Inside it's all oak-paneled and ironworked and cork-
floored, just like the real thing.

What the families then did was to import not just the husk of high
culture as perceived by robber barons, but the actual stuff. These people
had exquisite taste (or good agents, or more probably both), and the collection almost overflows with the best artists, both American (Homer,
Bierstadt, Sargent, Cassatt . . .) and European (Millet, Van Gogh, Corot,
Breton . . .). With the exception of a few paintings in the cellar, however,
there is not much southern art.

But what I found most extraordinary is that tucked in with all this
high-culture paint and plaster was an exquisite collection of English silver that came not from plundering timber, but from the local newspaper
publisher probably plundering advertisers. Thomas and Harriet Gibbons, co-owners of the *Laurel Leader-Call*, quietly collected more than a

hundred objects of Georgian silver (including tea caddies, tea- and cof-feepots, baskets, entrée dishes, salvers, baby rattles . . .). They knew what they were doing; all the prestigious names are there (Plummer, Bate-man, Scofield), and I couldn't help but wonder what breakfast was like at the Gibbons household. Or better yet, teatime.

Of course there are books and prints and all manner of stuff (like a massive collection of baskets) one associates with museums, but still, finding this in Laurel, Mississippi, home to squirrel dogs and the Free County of Jones, is a shock. It is definitely not so-so. But this was, in fact, for a long time the only high-art museum in Mississippi. There are no video displays, no interactive exhibits, no audio tours, no buttons for the kiddies to push, and, alas, not many visitors.

Maybe the shock of the collection is mitigated by remembering that when you first walk into the museum, right behind the omnipresent museum gift shop, is one of the rooms from the old Rogers house next door. It fairly reeks of Anglophilia, complete with a three-quarter suit of armor, leatherbound books running up to the ceiling, and that gar-ish flocked reddish wallpaper. It's dark: polished wainscoting and ma-hogany tables and big stuffed chairs. Ancestor paintings on the wall, no landscapes or still images. These timber barons were really just the new planter class. King cotton, king timber. Same slave cabins out back. The white-suited Confederate planter with the cane had been replaced by the pin-striped investor with the calculator. But, as we saw in Thomas-ville, what was being aped was not the culture of the Old South but of Olde England.

If the North won the war and the South won Reconstruction, then capitalism won the rest. All around the museum the old, stately houses and even the nearby double-pen cabins are being taken over by a new influx of workers from Mexico. As the museum docent whispered to us, the browns are willing to do the work blacks won't do. They live four or five families piled in together with all their cars out front. We drove around. She was right. They have come up along El Camino East/West Corridor to work the new cotton/timber: chicken farms and transformer factories. It's doubtful, however, that the poultry processors and battery magnates are much interested in uplifting Laurel culture.

You Must Be Born Again

To see the real Laurel culture, the real white Laurel culture, or, better yet, the really white Laurel culture, I decided to go to church. I was in the heart of the Bible Belt, the place where historian John Shelton Reed observed that even folks who don't go to church know what church they're not going to. Some religious observers have contended that Deep Dixie is the most self-consciously religious section not just of the United States, but of the Western world. Only parts of Islam exceed its fervor. I don't know. But I know this: if you want to understand the South, you should exit the museum and enter the church.

In the spirit of the religious endeavor, let me first make a confession. I like going to southern churches. I started churchgoing about a decade ago as I became intrigued by American marketing. One of the base points in selling is that the closer your product is to that of your competitors, the more important narrative separation will become. Bottlers of water do a lot of marketing because the product is pretty much interchangeable. Ditto brewers of beer, soapmakers, long-distance telephone suppliers, computer chip makers, airline companies, and the like. You drive the nameplate, as they say, not the car.

So here's the religious product from a marketing point of view: it (1) does everything, (2) costs nothing, (3) is available 24/7, (4) comes with a lifetime warranty, and (5) is protected from competition by the state. This last point is crucial because, unlike in most every other country, there is no national supplier, no Church of America as there is a Church of England, the Scandinavian Lutheran Church, or the Holy Roman Catholic Church in France, Spain, and Italy. The First Amendment sees to it that every denomination in the United States must scramble for believers by telling a slightly different story about the same product. And indeed they do.

Consider that in 1900 there were 330 different religious groups; now there are more than two thousand doing business. This happens only in America. And it is not hard to explain. We have learned how to buy and sell almost anything: hospital care, art, education, philanthropy, quilts, collateralized debt obligations; you name it, and you'll soon find a market trading it. Everything goes to market. Why should religion be any different? There is a famous quote, so on-point that it has lost its specific source, though it is attributed to Richard Halverson, a former chaplain of the United States Senate: "In the beginning the church was a fellowship of men and women centering on the living Christ. Then the church moved to Greece, where it became a philosophy. Then it moved to Rome, where it became an institution. Next, it moved to Europe, where it became a culture. And, finally, it moved to America, where it became an enterprise."

It's in this context that the Southern Baptists are so interesting. No one scrambles better, competes more, or has had better success. First, they have a very informal organization with little top-down control. Once you believe that the Bible is inerrant and that Baptists know how to read it, the only question is your conversion—when and where.

Any male can become a Baptist minister, and anyone can open a Baptist church. That's why there are all kinds of Baptist subsets offering this conversion experience (Primitive, Missionary, Free Will, General, Regular, Hard Shell, Independent . . .), but the general group most represented along U.S. 84 is the Southern Baptist Convention (SBC). The SBC is the biggest U.S. Protestant group, with a reported membership of about 17 million.

They do almost no media advertising. There is no multimillion-dollar TV campaign like those of the other denominations (especially the Methodists, Presbyterians, Episcopalians, and Lutherans). When I started my trip, I thought I'd do a section on signage. What do signs say in the Deep South? What I found out was that, with the exception of places where the interstates bisected U.S. 84, there were very few signs along the road. And of the signs we saw, by far the most common were for this or that Baptist church. These were not the marquee signs with the clever sayings like "No God, No Peace. Know God, Know Peace" or "CH--CH; What's Missing? U R." What we saw were no-nonsense signs. *Jesus Loves You* or *Jesus Is the Answer*, and here's the Baptist church.

Every single town we went through had a big First Baptist Church downtown (red brick, white columns, little sign) and then a ringlet of other suppliers, most of whom had split and resplit, forming competing delivery services of the same product. As the Southern Baptists are the first to tell you, the splits are not for doctrinal reasons but because somebody gets annoyed with the minister's wife or the choice of altar flowers and off they go to "plant" a new church.

The real reason I like to go to this denomination is because everything is focused on the conversion story, and every SBC service uses this event as the selling pivot. The actual event is called the "altar call," and it comes at the end of every service as new converts come forward, or tired believers get to be charged up. For 1,700 years, the Christian church had thrived without this call forward. Such a practice was never used by Jesus or His apostles. Ironically, this is another northern invention like "Way Down upon the Swanee River" and "Dixie." The altar call was an innovation developed by Charles Grandison Finney, a Presbyterian preacher in upstate New York in the 1830s.

The Baptist church, especially the Southern Baptists, hijacked the altar call and made it a standard part of the service. Preachers like D. L. Moody, Billy Sunday, and especially Billy Graham were to use its methods to bring thousands forward at the close of their services. In the trade, the altar call is also called "dragging the net," and it's this that I go to the Baptist church (and the Pentecostal churches) to see. Can the minister do it? Can he close the sale? All I ask is that the church be big enough so I don't get caught up in the net.

I picked one at random and on February 6, 2009, I went to Salem Heights Baptist Church, located on what the church calls Glory Hill right on U.S. 84 outside Laurel. Out front is a large alpha-numeric sign with the slogan "The Difference Is Worth the Distance." The church has all the accouterments of the modern large Baptist church: huge video screens suspended from the ceiling, comfy seating, pin-drop-accurate sound system so you can hear every sound (especially the preacher's breathing), an amplified band, and a sound-and-light production center up in the balcony. That's where I like to sit because you not only get the best view, but you also can see what the congregation is doing.

Before the service starts there is a time for fellowship and a lot of handshaking and, especially for me, a bit too much welcoming and eagerness. My wife, Mary, doesn't like this part of the service, so she stayed out in the View. Salem Heights Baptist was an established congregation, and I don't think they see many new faces, so I'm a little overwhelmed by the open-armed welcome. I try to act small and am saved by the house lights going down and the video screens coming alive. I scoot upstairs.

First off, there is a little prepackaged show called *Imagine Yourself Debt-Free* telling you that the Financial Peace University is standing by to help educate you to organize your money exactly "the way Jesus would like." All you need do is fill out the questionnaire and someone from the church will come calling.

Over the screens in huge letters is this: You Must Be Born Again. The ad for financial salvation is over, and the little orchestra starts to play. I like this part because you can get a sense of the audience demographics from their musical preferences. Sometimes it's lite rock, but here it's sentimental music from the 1950s. No dolorous hymns. Sometimes we sing along, following words flashed on those screens. I look around. A lot of what are sarcastically called "Q-tips," or white-haired members, are attending. There's a choir, mostly women, behind the minister and the easy-listening music goes on for quite a while. An elderly deacon comes up to the balcony to tell me that I don't have to sit up here, that I might be more comfortable downstairs, but I say no thanks, I'm comfy.

From where I sit it looks like a convention center downstairs. The church is all white walls and plush green seats and is really clean. There's not an icon in the place, just some blue stained-glass windows. Behind the lectern are two huge white armchairs that look a little like thrones.

But here's the most striking sight. I've been to many Baptist churches. Admittedly I have never been to an all-black church, in part because I think my white skin would make things uncomfortable for the members. Sometimes, as in Orlando, Florida, the church has been about half black and half white. Often in white churches you'll see a few black faces as I did two weeks earlier at CrossPointe Baptist Church in Valdosta, Georgia. But here on Glory Hill in the Salem Heights Baptist Church, there was not a single black face in the entire congregation. This place is completely milk white.

Singing and announcements over, Rev. D. J. Benson, pastor, begins the service. It's pretty standard. He looks like a bulldog in a dark suit all buttoned up. And he behaves a bit like a bulldog, saying that we are being persecuted for our faith, that we need to prepare ourselves for the

downturn that has happened (Obama? the financial market?), that people want us to change and give over to their ways, that we have to realize
that when you are right, people always go out of their way to try to make
you wrong. "We must be prepared to fight, right church?" he says.

We also hear about Shadrach, Meshach, and Abednego from the
Book of Daniel and realize how close it is to our very own times. Pastor
Benson looks us in the eye and says, "You will be tested by fire. You can
look forward to it!" A little shudder. But not to worry. You have been
saved. You are "tea-bags . . . only good when heated up." The water will
be boiling soon.

This audience has heard it all before. There is a lot of "bless us" delivered from the lectern and some "isn't that right, church?" that merits
a quiet "amen." Now it's time to drag the net and everyone knows it.
Things turn hushed. From where I am, I can see maybe just two people
lining up to move to the altar. Now is the time to come forward. House
lights dim. The mini-orchestra, especially the piano, starts to play soft
music around just a few chords. This will continue for about five minutes, and I sit there waiting to see what happens. Nothing.

I notice the deacon has reappeared in the balcony and the three guys
who run the sound-and-light show near me are looking over at me. I
panic. Are they waiting for me? I slowly shake my head, and they turn
away as if in prayer. Once they're out of sight, I slowly get up and inch
to the door, then skedaddle as quietly as I can down the plush green car-
peted stairs, out through the side door, and rush back to my wife, who is
playing sudoku in the View.

A Tenth of a Degree

We hotfoot it out of town and head into the great vastness on the X axis
that is the Mississippi Delta. I felt a bit like Huckleberry Finn escaping
the clutches of Aunt Polly. We zipped past Prentiss, renowned, at least
to the WPA writers, for being the first town in the state to vote against
the legalization of beer after the repeal of Prohibition, as well as against
round dancing in the community center funded by WPA assistance. This
is clearly hostile territory.

We headed to camp at Monticello on the banks of the Pearl River, but even that looks a little bleak, so we handed ourselves over to Cecil, the disembodied voice of the Garmin, to take us to Lake Lincoln State Park. We should have known by the *Lincoln* that this was not going to be an easy destination.

The trip took forever. Cecil took us over back roads, each one getting narrower and narrower. We never lost faith, reminding each other that if Cecil had found the only package store in Monroeville, Alabama, he could certainly find Lake Lincoln in Wesson, Mississippi. We should have known that things were going to get a bit complex when he took us through a town called Sontag. In his clipped English accent he assured us we should stay on West Smith Ferry Road, then turn on to Athens Trail NE, then turn again to Heucks Retreat Road, and each time the road became more and more of a pathway and less and less of a thoroughfare. Finally, just as we were about to despair, there it was, the ranger station on a main road—Lake Lincoln Drive—coming in from the south.

We were clearly frazzled. Why didn't Cecil take this road? Our bewilderment must have shown because, without missing a beat, the ranger smiled and said, "You look as if you came using GPS." Yes, we admitted. "Oh," she said, "that never works. The park's location is off by a tenth of a degree." I thought it a telling remark, a motto for my trip thus far. If only I could understand just a bit more of the South, I'd be able to drive direct to Coushatta, confident.

Expectations of Natchez

As soon as I began to plan my trip, whenever I would tell someone of the algebra of my quest, they would invariably say, oh, just wait 'til you get to Natchez. Assumption being that Natchez would somehow solve everything, the Deep South would become shallow and fathomable. After all, Natchez has a copyrighted slogan: Where the Old South Still Lives. All I would have to do was look around and things would fall in place. I was certainly aware as the road flattened out across the ancient floodplain that there had to be something at the end of this. Maybe not a rainbow, but at least a vista.

I'm not sure what I pictured, but as I think about it now, Natchez was becoming the City on the Hill. In my mind's eye I was seeing this magical kingdom high above the gray river, cast in the light of brilliant magnolias, filled with oak-alleyed mansions, a few Ava Gardners in hoop skirts, lots of Bombay gin, and some sage old planters who remembered my great-grandfather and wanted to tell me about him. I felt like Robin, the kid in Hawthorne's "My Kinsman, Major Molineux," who was going into the big city to find his place in the world. I was about to find out the truth about my kinsman. No doubt about it, as we were nearing Natchez, U.S. 84 was taking on the decidedly golden tint of a yellow brick road.

I was being set up for a fall. I should have known. After all, I've read the Hawthorne story many times. And disillusion came right at the get-go in the visitors' center. As we burst into this cement bunker overlooking the gun-metal gray river, the first thing we saw was a large flat-screen TV blaring, you guessed it, Fox News. Here I was all set to enter the world of mystery and forbidden knowledge and it was just more of those squawky blondes and loud bullyboys talking about Michelle Obama's biceps and her husband presiding over the end of the world (which will happen right after the next commercial).

I was relieved to see that a few yards past the big screen there was a small classroom amphitheater showing a movie about Natchez. Now this was more like it. We gleefully paid $1.50 apiece, senior rate, and were the only ones in the show. The ticket taker told us to take our time. The show was just for us.

Now we know why. What we saw in 2009 was a DVD from the 1990s done in the style of the 1960s praising Natchez from the 1980s. We saw lots of fuzzy pictures of white kids at the Old South Ball, and then a black face, pan across some pictures of pom-pom'd cheerleaders, and then a black face, some reenactments of drinking mint juleps on the veranda, and then a black face, some still-pictures shot through gauze of the antebellum downtown, and then a black face, some hot-air balloons floating across the river, and then an Indian face. We learned nothing about Natchez, but a lot about affirmative action as understood by the Natchez visitors' center.

We stocked up on glossy pamphlets (mansions galore, riverbank saloons, ghost tours, cotton gins, indigo factories, juke joints, garden tours, steamboats, catfish farms, slave markets, and, of course, RV parks), my wife left a note about removing the television or at least changing the channel, and skulked back to the View. I should have asked for our three dollars back for our tickets to the retro PR movie. Clearly Natchez was not going to measure up. Like Robin, at the end of the story, I had seen enough.

Southern Honor

Worse, the one thing I wanted to see in Natchez had changed sides of the river. Thanks to some tinkering by the Army Corp of Engineers, the famous sandbar dueling site was now in Louisiana. At this sandbar James Bowie became a national icon. For those who passed through their teenage traumas in the 1950s, the name of Jim Bowie has almost the resonance of Davy Crockett. Here's why: every boy goes through a knife period. That's why there were all those knives at the Rattlesnake Roundup. It's the one object you can have that not only extends your puny power, but which also gets immediately taken away from you at school. Or at home. Shades of my great-grandfather's sword.

Jim Bowie had this knife. It was about a foot long. And of course as a kid I wanted one. It was so big you had to wear it in a holster and, truth be told, you couldn't do much damage because it weighed a ton. You certainly couldn't take it to school—you could barely carry it out of your room. If you wanted to see it in action, the fledgling network ABC ran a television series called *The Adventures of Jim Bowie* in the late 1950s. Or, better yet, you could see it in action in John Wayne's *The Alamo* (1960), in which Richard Widmark as Bowie waves the cleaver at various people, mostly Mexicans. Until they were kicked out by the park department, collectors with metal detectors have sought the original knife that supposedly still lies buried in the sand around the Alamo.

Mr. Bowie spent some time with his meat axe in Natchez. On September 19, 1827, there was one of many duels fought north of Natchez. Mr. Bowie went as an observer. The duel proved inconclusive, and as the duelists prepared to take their honor home intact, a donnybrook broke out among the spectators, and big Jim was wounded. Bad mistake. He pulls out the gargantuan chopper and charges the guy who shot him. All hell breaks out. People are stabbed, some shot, some knifed, and for a while at least, Mr. Bowie has a sword stuck in his chest. He pulls it out with a flourish. The Battle of the Sandbar didn't last long, only about ten minutes, but two men died and four were wounded, with one death and a wounding attributable to Bowie and his hunk of iron.

But the scene becomes important because the newspapers spread the story, and "cuts," or engraved images of the knife, enter the world of boys' reading material. Mr. Bowie reprises this scene a few years later in Texas, when he is attacked by three desperadoes. Honor besmirched, out comes the massive shiv, and one man is almost beheaded, another slit across the midriff, and the third has his skull cracked. When you go to a toy store and see those large rubber knives, you know that the Bowie legacy is alive and well. It's not really a knife so much as a portable guillotine.

The sandbar event of course has all the ingredients I am interested in. It's superviolent, all male, based to some extent on the concept of honor, and it doesn't seem to alarm the authorities. True, it's not Coushatta, in the sense that it's really not planned and no Yankees are involved, but it does show how tribal groups of men can explode in southern culture and how they get remembered.

There's no doubt Natchez, under all the wisteria, was a very violent town. All through the nineteenth century, traders on flatboats would float their wares, mostly tobacco and cotton, downriver, sell out in Natchez, and then head back north by horseback and foot. Since they were carrying cash on the return trip, they were often set on by thieves. Hence the development of a safe passage, the Natchez Trace, back up to Nashville. The same would happen to the west, as cattle were driven from Texas across Louisiana to Natchez, where they would be slaughtered and their meat sent south on steamboat or barge. Cattle drivers were also harvested by ruffians as they returned home. But there was no safe passage home. U.S. 84 was the route they took, and it became decidedly more violent as it crossed Louisiana.

Under-the-Hill: Where Fun Begins and Segregation Ends

The place where much of this violence would take place in Natchez was called Under-the-Hill, the dusty riverbank where the steamboats docked and the traders of various commodities were paid off. Predictably this was where the gamblers, loose women, saloon keepers, thieves, and cut-throats plied their craft. Not much has changed. Now cemented in at the steamboat landing is the Isle of Capri, a faux side-wheeler. If you want to be fleeced, all you have to do is go aboard.

Desperate to make money in the late 1980s and aware of what was happening in Louisiana, the State of Mississippi decided to allow gambling on the river. Why should New Orleans be able to shake down tourists and Natchez be denied? The key concept was "on the river," as the early boats actually left the shore. Thus the state could say there was no gambling on state land. But no one liked this; the gamblers would run out of money and want to go home, and the boat owners were having to be sure their rigs were shipshape, which was expensive.

So laws were passed essentially giving the captain power to decide whether he felt it safe to shove off or not. If he wanted to keep his job, he felt it was safer to stay tied up. Soon the jig was up, and a new generation of casinos tricked out as boats were built; they just sat on the shore and pretended to be nautical.

To get to the Isle of Capri we had to park in a special lot and ride a shuttle bus down to the "boat." Near where we parked the View were much bigger vans from places like "Liberty Community Living Center," which were dutifully ferrying their charges into the world Under-the-Hill. The shuttle bus was about 70 percent black, and as we drove through the parking lot proper, I noticed that almost all the cars were from Mississippi. This was a happy trip, everyone chatting and looking excited.

We eagerly disembarked the shuttle bus clutching our purses, crossed the concrete gangplank, and entered "The Place Where Fun Begins." Cheerless doesn't describe it. The place was packed with slot machines, card tables, craps, roulette wheels, and video poker. Not a window to be seen, no clocks anywhere, fresh air pumped in, and that high-pitched background sound mimicking occasional machine payouts.

The black and white faces now took on a more dour look as we were seeing people who had been in *the place where fun begins* for some time. But what was also noteworthy was that here real integration has taken place. With the exception of the money-changing bank behind thick glass, the people tending the bar, the tables, the security, the hosting, and the picking-up were, like the gamblers, both races. Here, at last, one part of the City on the Hill was in place. Who would have known that Natchez, behind New Orleans, had been the second-largest slave market in the Old South?

We didn't stay long. That calliope circus noise was distracting, as it is meant to be, and I wanted out. So back across the gangplank and into the shuttle bus. Our bus mates were glum, quiet, and still integrated. Back to the retirement home to rest. Mississippi now ranks second in the world in terms of casino space. They have hit the jackpot. And maybe, in a strange way, slot machines, cards, and dice have resolved the dilemma we saw in Alabama, namely, that both races have learned too well how to stay apart. On the Isle of Capri everyone was willing to come together. The gaming economy was doing what the market economy can't do. Certainly, as I had seen in the Salem Heights Baptist Church, the salvation economy wasn't going to get them together either. Maybe, as I remembered the granite war memorial back at the Clarke County Historical Museum, we all finally give up handed-down prejudice as we bow before the Grim Reaper and Lady Luck.

5

Louisiana Gumbo

One of these days the people of Louisiana are going to get
good government—and they aren't going to like it.

—HUEY LONG

Truth be told, we didn't even stay in Natchez. Ever the suckers
for a good advertisement, we stayed across the river in Vidalia, Louisiana, and commuted. River View RV Park & Resort
claims on the Web that it is "The Finest RV Park on the Mighty Mississippi" and the place to stay while visiting Natchez. I didn't really calcu-
late what "*on* the Mighty Mississippi" might mean. River View may well
be the *only* RV park *on* the river. No one in their right mind builds an
RV park on the edge of the Mississippi because the Mississippi might
soon be seeping into your RVs. What we got was a concrete pad on the
floodplain, a few scraggly trees, and next door a shipping terminal for
some kind of toxic chemicals. I didn't care. I loved watching the barges
lumbering by all day and night. To get a site with a barge view for a View
barge cost five dollars extra, but it was worth it.

Vidalia has done a pretty good job of co-opting Natchez's thunder.
Not only do they have the place to stay while visiting Natchez, but they
also hijacked the dueling sandbar of Jim Bowie fame. Insult to injury,
they even incorporated the Bowie knife into the town logo. The V of Vidalia is made of Bowie knives. I was glad to see they made no attempt to
steal the onion from Vidalia, Georgia.

We had an informative dinner at Nikki's right on U.S. 84. The place was full of plump good ol' boys and their stout women who love them, and they all assured me there was absolutely nothing to see in Vidalia. They were friendly and they were talking politics and eating the best gumbo I've ever had. They were giggling the way big red-faced men do and telling jokes, and I strained to eavesdrop. They were hoping that some of the bailout money would come their way, and they were curious about how Obama was going to "nigger-rig" the economy.

The N-word, even in this context that Willie Campbell had prepared me for, jolted a little, especially because it was being used in front of young blacks who were also working and eating in Nikki's. We would hear a lot more of the unself-conscious use of the term in Louisiana than we had heard across the rest of the South. I'm not sure why. In the world I live in, the N-word has such a sting because we have all given it bite, but clearly here in Vidalia it's like the Georgia onion. At least to whites.

One of the big 'uns leaned over and said to us, there is something we should see. Up the road in Ferriday we should see the music museum and talk with Jerry's sister. I had planned to go to the museum, but I didn't know about the sister. The Delta Music Museum was certainly on the itinerary because it celebrated three of my favorite figures: Jerry Lee Lewis, Jimmy Swaggart, and Mickey Gilley. They are cousins.

Jerry, Mickey, Jimmy, and Frankie Jean Lewis

Ferriday is a dump. In fact, this whole side of the Mississippi River is a desolate place. Even Ulysses S. Grant had trouble spending the winter here as he moved south, hoping to cross the river below Vicksburg and then double back. There's just nothing to it. The land is flatter than Mississippi and it floods more. All up this western side of the river there were huge cotton and indigo plantations, but because of the flooding the planters did not live here. Unlike us, they lived in Natchez and commuted to Louisiana. We were repeatedly told that before the Civil War there were more millionaires here than anywhere else in the South. You certainly wouldn't know it by what's there now.

Ferriday claims to have produced more famous people per square foot than any other American small town. And the Delta Music Museum honors more than the cousins: journalist Howard K. Smith and socialite Ann Boyar Warner (wife of movie man Jack) as well as some other musicians and politicians. But it's essentially a shrine to the cousins wedged into an old post office.

What it really is, I think, is a shrine to powers of cultural miscegenation. For it's here that African American culture moved through redneck culture and, thanks to a juke joint, Haney's Big House, made it into the vocal chords (and hair and noses) of the Lewis/Gilley family. I don't know how else to explain it because if you listen to the music of these three men, you can hear a lilting breathiness that you hear in black women's voices. It's almost a cooing sound these men make that is so similar and so compelling. It's joyful. You can hear it in Elvis too.

As you enter the museum there's a plaster-of-Paris cast of the three cousins singing around a piano. Mickey is on one side, Jimmy is at the piano, and Jerry is on the far side. Supposedly when Jimmy Swaggart saw it, he said that it represented two sinners on the side and a saint (himself) in the middle. We were assured by our kindly docent that a better description would be the good, the bad, and the ugly.

I grew up with these three men sweating on the television, and they are, for me, beyond judgment. The State of Louisiana, which underwrites the museum, seems to agree. Big deal if the minister does a bit of whoring or if Jerry married his pubescent cousin and was kicked out of England for it. They have those divine voices. If the South is an aural culture not a visual culture, Ferriday is one of the broadcasting towers of that sound.

Our guide told us we should go up past the Lewis home because Jerry's sister sometimes gives a tour of the homestead. It's right next to U.S. 84. But we should be careful because the sister was a handful. So we drove the rig up the road to what looked like a nondescript wooden house. But that's only if you didn't look carefully. On closer look, you'll see that the house is connected to an ancient drive-through liquor store and you can still see the sign: *Terrell's Drive Through* across the second story. And the yard is festooned with small signs and objects that make no sense at all. For instance, there are slabs of marble laid down side by side and what look like small stacks of discarded stuff in tied bundles.

I guided the View over to have a better look, and out of the house pops this slight energetic woman about my age who asks if we want the tour, and when we say yes, she tells us she has to get ready and bounces back into the house. As opposed to most southerners, she talks fast like a Yankee, in almost a stutter, but from the first time she opens her mouth you can hear those vocal chords. She sounds just like the boys, all that warm air coming out with the sounds.

Her name is Frankie Jean Lewis and she's about ten years younger than her famous cousins. She grew up in the house, and she wants to show us around but before we get the tour, she wants us to know that life is hard and the utility bills are high and there's so much to do and none of it's free and things are getting worse and worse and. . . . I could listen to this voice forever. It's just such a sexy purr. But I figure she wants to know if we are going to make a contribution before she begins the tour so I assure her I'm good for it. That has a calming effect, and she asks our names and in we go. She will call us by our complete names for the next hour.

The parlor, I guess you'd call it, is a large room with a concrete floor. It's dark and piled to the ceiling with objects. There's a wrought-iron outdoor dining table with chairs, a tree trunk with knives and a hatchet stuck in it, an old piano covered with one of those felt hangings with a tiger on a black background, a bar complete with foot rail, pictures of various saints, a painting of Jerry looking a little more dazed than usual, books piled up, a Christmas tree covered in a doily, drinking glasses of various colors, and some old telephones. The room is an explosion in a junk store. With one exception: there is absolutely no dust or dirt. It's an immaculate mess.

When I ask about the organizing principle for the room decoration, Frankie Jean says *plunking*. I look puzzled and she explains, she plunks something down. As she is saying this, she is leaning over to pick up some barely visible dust. I tell her I've been looking for decorative arts in the rural South and haven't found much because it's all here in her house. She coos a bit. I can't help myself; I'm captivated by that husky voice. I could listen to her all day, but I look over at Mary and it's clear that she can't. Frankie Jean says she is the only recycler in town, and that's why much of this stuff is here. She is recycling it. That's why the marble slabs are out front in the yard. She is planning to cover the entire yard with those slabs. That saves on cutting the grass.

We follow some painted footmarks on the floor up a few steps into the next rooms. There's not an empty space anywhere. Everything is covered and stuffed. "Please, no photos," she politely asks. Even the windows are blocked out with stuff. There's no outside light coming in, so in places it's totally dark. The walls are covered with paper. Sometimes it's Jerry's early sermons, sometimes it's cutouts from magazines, sometimes autographed photos from newscasters, and sometimes it's Frankie Jean's artwork. I look more carefully. There's a Williams-Sonoma catalog framed. I don't dare ask why. There are more upright pianos scattered about, sofas, chairs, old tables in no particular order, just *plunked*. In each of the little rooms there's a fan running and, although it's not the least hot, it certainly is windy. I mention this and she agrees. On the floor she has painted a rug.

Although I found Frankie Jean delightful, it was clear she was living in a slightly different place from the rest of us. All the time she was dusting and talking nonstop, telling us about how she sleeps like a fireman (with her clothes on), or how she has a friend who sends her cleaning supplies from Connecticut, how she never hears from Jerry, how she supports the museum with no help from her siblings. I realized from Mary's rolled eyes we had to go, and I started to inch for the door and follow those painted footprints back outside. Frankie Jean asked me if I wanted to see her artwork and, ever the fool, I said I certainly did. Out came a raft of paper, each sheet carefully marked and each loaded to the margins with colorful images. Which did I want to buy? Did I want to buy? Of course I did.

And I did. It's a very nice collage. In the background is a carefully drawn ranch house with a tree in front. Right in the middle is a little stump with "Visit" stuck on top of it. Then a black roadway in front, and in front of that a green and blue dabbed lawn going over the edge toward the viewer. Peering over the house is Jerry Lee himself. To his side is a new moon in the sky. On the mailbox, center left, is "all Killer" cut out and pasted, and then sprinkled around the scene are cutouts of Jerry and young women. Over near the window of the ranch house is a little sticker in ballpoint pen saying "Elmo." Not an inch of the paper is empty.

We exited, having made our small contribution and having spent some time in the museum gift shop buying the artwork. We were start-

Untitled collage, c. 2008, Frankie Jean Lewis
In possession of the author

ing to move out of the parking space when Frankie Jean comes running
out of the house with "some more mementoes for you, Jim and Mary
Twitchell." She hands it to me through the open window. I thank her
and drive slowly off. It's a potholder that says, "In Loving Memory to
You from My Mother's Kitchen" and a copy of *Happiness* magazine from
Covin's Pharmacy. Inside is the television schedule for October 20, 2007.

The Jena 6

It started to rain. The rain made going to Frogmore Plantation impossible as the place was drenched. I wanted to see it because it is a working
cotton plantation open to the public, but no work was being done. Only
the place's namesakes were happy. So we just drove on to Jena.

The road was crowded with trucks until we came to where new
Route 28 meets U.S. 84. Then U.S. 84 suddenly emptied. Highway 28,
built in the mid-1950s and called the Korean War Veterans Highway, effectively drains off all the east-west traffic from U.S. 84, leaving all the
towns—notably Jena and Winnfield—stranded. Only local traffic uses
this section of the road and perhaps that accounts for what happened to

Jena a few years ago. This part of U.S. 84 has become a world passed by and forgotten, almost.

The first thing you notice about Louisiana is they pronounce things differently. Jena was not pronounced Jenn-a but Jean-ah. Coushatta was pronounced Coo-shatta. Colfax was Coul-fax. And I won't even attempt Natchitoches. Since it was still raining, I decided to be brash and go to the town hall and ask for help. Almost all parish seats have a massive town hall/courthouse in the dead center, but Jena has a newish one-story brick office right on U.S. 84. I entered sopping wet. Inside was no visible mention of the Civil War or Reconstruction. Before me was the mayor's office. Did they have anyone who might show me Jena? I asked in my Yankee twang. The secretary just looked at me. I said it again, same response. You know, I said, show me around Jenn-a. Oh, Jean-ah, the secretary smiled.

Going into the mayor's office and asking for the grand tour is a little, what? Impolite Yankee. Pushy. Especially if the town is notorious. But it wasn't going to quit raining and I was desperate. I needed to see some signs of Louisiana violence: the famous tree that held the noose, the high school that was burned, and the courthouse that had become an emblem of what had been called "stealth racism." I wanted to see what was stealthy about this kind of racism; it seemed obvious. But, like the peanut factory in Blakely, this was hard to ask about straightaway so I explained my trip, that I was going to Coushatta, that I had been on U.S. 84 since the Okefenokee Swamp, and that I wanted to understand the ways of the Deep South.

There really is such a thing as southern hospitality. I had seen it every day from the way people gave directions, the way they offered to show you things, and the way they shared things. I was, of course, suspicious. Did it also include how they treated you as they were promising safe passage out of the state or right before they shot your arms off? Are they only hospitable when you aren't threatening? Is this hospitality the tribute deception pays to violence? Is it how they behave right before the slaughter begins?

The one secretary alerted another, and both of them started calling around to find me a guide. The florist couldn't do it (Valentine's Day tomorrow), the meter reader was out on his route, the doctor takes Friday off but couldn't be located. Finally the first secretary said her retired dad could help, but it would take him about an hour to get to town. He was a Jena native, had been in law enforcement, and knew everything about the town.

I said great and thanks and left to get the RV ready for spending the night. Jena doesn't have a real RV park, just some concrete pads near a motel. The motel has seen happier times, but it's the only one left since the bypass to Alexandria has been built. This also gave us time to study up on the Jena 6.

Here's the gist of what happened in 2007. Almost every fact is disputed but this one: school started in late August. Everything that I'm now about to say has been contradicted. Here goes. At an assembly a new student (black) asked if he could sit under the "white tree," an oak planted by one of the classes in the early 1960s. The assistant principal said you can sit wherever you want. A few days later, some (up to three) nooses appeared in that tree. The maintenance crew took them down before school started. Few students saw them, but some did.

School officials identified the three students (white) who put the nooses up and punished them with suspension. Their parents complained that the three kids really didn't appreciate how powerful the imagery was. Black parents said yes they did. The suspensions turned out to be something like house arrest, and the blacks were upset. In weeks to come, fights broke out at school and a fire was started that closed the school for a few days, but those events are claimed by some to be unconnected. Months later, in December, a fight broke out and a white student was so badly beaten by six blacks that he was taken to the hospital. Pictures were taken. He was really pummeled. The fight probably had no direct connection to the nooses. Six blacks were apprehended, taken downtown, booked, and charged not with assault but with attempted murder. Five were charged as adults.

When one of the blacks was found guilty on second-degree battery charges by an all-white jury, the tipping point was crossed, and Jena entered the national news cycle. Interestingly, the 150-person jury pool included fifty black citizens, none of whom showed up. The defense lawyer never challenged the jury selection, however.

The *Jena 6* had become a proverbial feeding frenzy, the racial equivalent of the perfect storm. It had everything: nooses, hanging tree, school fire, beatings, all-white jury, and harsh sentencing that implied lynching, thereby invoking the image that started it off: nooses in the hanging tree. Best yet, it took place in the Deep South. The *Chicago Tribune* was the first national paper with the story, then the *New York Times* carried a version as well as an op-ed piece by Orlando Patterson, NPR sent its microphones and hushed voices, and soon Jesse Jackson and Al Sharpton arrived, complete with their entourages and megaphones. Buses of protesters to follow.

Jena became a culture whirlpool. Rock star David Bowie poured ten thousand dollars into the legal defense fund; John Mellencamp released a song and video called "Jena," with lyrics such as "Jena, take your nooses down"; an episode of the *Salt-N-Pepa Show* on VH1 was filmed at the Jena rally; and YouTube and blogs featured the amateur contributions to mass outrage. Jena was prime subject matter in a BBC documentary, *Race Hate in Louisiana*. All over the world, Jena was becoming emblematic, a condensation of toxic *southern* racism, a brand of Way Down South in Dixie.

On September 20, 2007, on the date when the sentencing of one of the kids was to take place, some fifteen thousand to twenty thousand demonstrators appeared in the cramped downtown. However, since then, poof! the Jena 6 have gone into the dim embers of media firestorms. Charges have been reshuffled, some dropped, a few kids served short time in custody, five finally pleaded no contest to misdemeanor simple battery and were sentenced to seven days' probation. Only one kid served serious jail time. He pleaded guilty to second-degree battery and was sentenced to eighteen months. Some of the kids have left town, and, most depressingly, a few of them have become mixed up with the law again. Jena 6 started so simple and became so complicated; then, almost overnight, other stories pushed it aside.

We get the RV all squared away and tidied up for our tour guide and in he comes, driving a cherry red Ford 150 pickup. He's about five foot eleven in cowboy boots, short white hair, and wearing a neat brown shirt with someone's initials on the chest. In fact, he's looking like the Marlboro man of dignified retirement age. He introduces himself as Carl

Smith and, getting into the front passenger seat of the View, says his daughter said we wanted a tour. Just what sort of tour did we have in mind? I explain what I'm up to, that I am interested in what happened in Colfax and Coushatta a century ago, and he remembers as a kid he heard that some men from Jena had to go over to Colfax to help put down that uprising. He knows nothing about Coushatta, however, and I didn't think it wise to tell him what side I was on.

As we drive around town, I notice how everyone seems to be waving at him, both races. He remembers where everything was, the old banks, the old grocery stores, the old motels, the sawmills, the train depot, and I casually ask if the recent unpleasantness has scarred the town. No, he says, it all went away as quick as it came. But he says it had an effect on him. I look over, and he's a little wistful. "I retired after it," he says. "I was real tired. I was the sheriff."

That set me into a panic because I had just read some of the newspaper reports, and I knew that almost every fact was contested, but I didn't know what to ask—number of nooses, reason for the fire, who did what, his role in the trial, the media explosion. I remember the cotton gin manager back in Blakely saying, "Y'all are rude and we are all ignorant." I certainly didn't want to piss off the sheriff by asking about things he didn't want to talk about. I kept my mouth shut. Worse, instead of asking the appropriate follow-up questions, every time we went around a corner I'd lean over to look at his shirt. I believe the ex-sheriff of this small southern town had YSL initials on the chest. Yves St. Laurent.

Carl Smith was more than happy to talk about the "unpleasantness." In fact, a year or so after the event, it was clear that his life in retirement had become almost too quiet. And it was also clear that he was especially proud of a fact that had never been reported. During the entire "media circus," as he called it, not a single arrest was made. Even though thirty thousand people were in town (his figure was a little high), his men did a great job of keeping things under control. And not because his life was made easy. Busloads of protesters had come in from as far away as LA and Philadelphia. Parking was so bad that people had to park way out of town and walk in. They were upset, "spoil'n for action." There could have been a riot.

The whole matter was unfair, Sheriff Smith said. The event of "school violence," of that white kid getting "hurt bad," was essentially overlooked because of those nooses. There were eight attackers, not six, but once the *Jena 6* term was coined, "it made no difference what the truth was." He didn't think the fight in which the white kid was badly beaten had anything to do with the nooses. When Mary asked what the fight was about if not the nooses, Carl said, "Don't know it's ever been asked." It was just assumed. The attackers "bonded out" so no one did much jail time. Furthermore, he asserted, the school fire had nothing to do with the incident; it had to do with an attempt to destroy grades. In fact, he added, kids of both races were caught using their cell phones to capture images of the arson and send them along to their friends. It took a year to get all the evidence but, of course, he said, *that* wasn't reported.

Carl said he went to that high school in 1968 and groups intermingled but sat apart at lunch. At that time, he said, "we didn't have many of the . . ." and he stopped and looked at Mary and me, "blacks." In fact, Louisiana didn't really integrate its schools until 1970, but the point was made. Then he said what I was to realize is the crucial observation: Jena was a *good* town. He said no more. He was saying something more than its behavior was good; he was alluding to its racial makeup. Jena is predominately white, about 80 percent. When towns move to 60/40, we were to learn, they become *bad,* and whites leave. Then, presumably, they get worse.

I asked about Jesse and Al, and he said they were "real gentlemen." Jesse was exhausted and wanted to rest up in the sheriff's office, and Al was an affable man, at least until he saw the lens of a camera. Al's people were "real pros," especially with the buses. They knew how to move the buses in and out. They had done it many times before. In all fairness, Carl said, the people who came were almost all well behaved because Jesse and Al exercised most of the control, not him. The Jena business community was upset that the crowd had been told not to buy anything from local stores. But other than that, the town "played its part."

As we drove by the high school, a large black man, who must have been a crossing guard, recognized Carl and started waving, and then the schoolkids did too. Carl pointed to where the tree had been and said it was too bad it was taken down—"it wasn't the tree's fault"—but that tree was coming down anyway to make room for an addition. It was impossible not to like Carl, and it was impossible not to sympathize with this little town that had been blown up in this massacre by media. But still, under it all, this was a scene of violence, real violence.

I couldn't get out of my mind that Carl remembered being told that men from Jena went across the forest in the 1870s to put down the "riot" in Colfax. I should have asked him if any went to clean out the carpetbaggers in Coushatta. Maybe that would have been a mistake. If Coushatta were happening today, how close would it be to Jena, not in violence but in narrative cover-up? Would the sheriff be claiming that this was a little problem in keeping a good town from going bad?

You Are My Sunshine

The rain had stopped when we left Jena, but I was in no hurry to cross the Kisatchie National Forest to the Red River valley. In fact, I was a little apprehensive. So up we went to Winnfield. Winnfield's great fame in the twentieth century was that it produced the populist politicians Huey and Earl Long. It also produced, or so we were told, Alabama's George Wallace. I found out later this was just a confusion of names. There was a George Wallace in Louisiana politics, but the confusion was purposeful. In some respects, this part of Louisiana is like the Free State of Jones in Mississippi and in some respects like Ferriday and its famous threesome. And in some respects, like Alabama.

We arrived on Saturday afternoon, and once again southern hospitality saved the day. The local museum was closed, but after we told the proprietress of the Pea Patch (a mall of knickknacks and art and antiques, many with a dollop of born-again Christianity) of our interest in the Deep South, she offered to call her cousin and have the Louisiana Political Museum opened up just for us. It was.

Again and again in Louisiana we heard that politics is just a game and these men were the best gamers of the system. Huey, the self-styled Kingfish, and one of his brothers, Earl, were masterful manipulators of public sentiment, often in the cause of violent redistribution and revenge. My favorite Huey story was that he had a famous "deduct box" near where public employees were paid. You were to put part of your paycheck in to protect your job. After he died, people furiously looked for the big deduct box that supposedly held all the booty. None was ever found. And Earl ("Vote for Uncle Earl. I ain't crazy" was his campaign slogan) asked to be buried in Winnfield in a spot that would be right under the kitchen sink of the family house. He said it was the only safe place he had ever known. The Longs were great performers of politics. They became larger-than-life vice characters, rather like Thanksgiving Day parade balloons.

I couldn't help but wonder if what I had seen in Jena, and what I knew happened a century ago across the forest along the Red River, was somehow connected to a strain of self-protection via charade, a game of let's pretend, that produced these belligerent puffer fish, the Longs. So just as adolescent boys play rough games like cops and robbers, just as they watch violent spectacle like professional wrestling and attend make-believe Rattlesnake Roundups, just as Mardi Gras seems to blow off excesses via spoof, so too does Louisiana politics sublimate and deflect the chaos and trauma that really have happened here.

This is a violent place, not just because of slavery, poverty, and the carpetbaggers but because there has been a never-ending jostling of groups hitting hard against each other. They don't seem to want to quit and make nice. Look at any list of the most violent states, and you'll see Louisiana in the top ten, and not for just a few years but for decades. Choose whatever metric you want: murder, rape, robbery, aggravated assault, burglary, motor-vehicle theft, you name it, and it's *not* chances are Louisiana will be in the top ten; it's Louisiana *is* in the top ten. I think what my kin experienced a century ago, and what happened a few years ago in Jena, and maybe even what we saw in Ferriday, are the results of a culture that can't quiet down, that cuts at the edges, that lives near the boiling point.

And, most important, Louisiana has adapted to frenzy. Politics here doesn't kiss and make up with violence; it stirs it up. And loves it. Because, get this: the *Washington Post* reports that the Sportsman's Paradise and Big Easy lead the nation in happiness ("Louisiana Tops Happiness Survey," January 3, 2010). The irony was not lost on us. Louisiana is a very happy place. You can feel it. The gumbo is just really hot.

I remember reading a passage in V. S. Naipaul's *A Turn in the South* (Knopf, 1989), essentially a book of conversations that Naipaul, an Indian-Jamaican, has with mostly middle-class American blacks in places like Atlanta, Charleston, Jackson, Nashville, and Chapel Hill. In Jackson, Mississippi, he talked with a white judge in his mid-eighties, who was explaining the peculiarity of southern rural violence. The judge recalls his country childhood:

> The closeness of that community, deprived and ill-educated, led to violence. People mightn't feel the need for promissory notes, and mightn't lock their doors, mightn't even have keys for some of the doors. But tempers could be quick. There were homicides, crimes of passion.
>
> They would just get angry, get into an argument, lose their temper. Some of them would be drunk. They would maybe be quarreling and have a fight, and somebody would get killed. They were slow to arouse, but when you get somebody like that angry somebody would get hurt. Otherwise, helpful people, lovely people. (200)

More than other states traversed by U.S. 84, Louisiana seems to have a higher octane of this pizzazz. It's more than being violent; it's accepting violence, even maybe liking it. It's entertaining, at least for some. For instance, I found it interesting that almost everyone we spoke to had an opinion about Huey's violent death. He was shot in the gut by either an upset doctor (Carl Weiss), his own bodyguards, or an agent of FDR. I wasn't really interested in who did him in, but in the fact that no one seemed to react to assassination as if it were out of the ordinary. "Of course he got shot, whaddaya expect?"

Violence is the cayenne pepper of this gumbo. As we drove down U.S. 84 in Jena, retired sheriff Smith commented on gunshot holes in the wall of a building and told the story of how they got there. When I asked him if this place was more violent than others, he said he didn't think so, at least not more than other places in this state. I asked how long it had been going on, and he said since the Texans first started driving cattle across the state to Natchez. There is no safe passage across Louisiana, no Natchez Trace.

What made this paradoxical is that after we spent time at the Louisiana Political Museum in Winnfield, we headed up to spend the night at the Jimmie Davis State Park. Mr. Davis was one of the most popular governors of Louisiana, serving two nonconsecutive terms (1944–48 and 1960–64). He supposedly wrote (or bought, it's not clear) the well-known song "You Are My Sunshine," which became one of the state songs of Louisiana in 1977. He composed it, he claimed, for his horse, a Palomino named Sunshine.

Louisianians loved that their governor felt so strongly about his horse. But my only feeling was, how about feeling that way about your fellow man? Clearly, as they used to say, there is a disconnect here, something is missing. In the Delta Music Museum I had seen a color picture of Mr. Davis leading Sunshine up the Capitol steps in Baton Rouge. He's taking the horse to visit his office because he wanted his horse to see where he worked. And perhaps sing him the song. I remember hearing somewhere that cultures deeply attached to loving animals often were not so deeply attached to loving humans. I wondered if that were true. Maybe brotherly love has been overhyped.

Biding My Time

I was still strangely anxious about crossing over to the Red River valley and visiting Coushatta and Colfax. I wasn't ready. I had hoped that by this time I would have understood the Deep South, or at least enough of the culture to sort through my feelings. I wasn't afraid of violence, but of the fact that I was going to be face to face with the descendants of that violence. They were not going to be remorseful; I now realized that. In fact, just the opposite. They would feel proud of what their violence wrought.

Looking at the townspeople of Dothan or Camden or Laurel or Jena, I had imagined that these were the people who had massacred my family and crippled my great-grandfather. Okay, I could handle that. I could imagine myself as them, as people who were distraught at being told what to do by some outsider, as people who just wanted things to be the way they were before all this "recent unpleasantness" had happened.

New Englanders would feel the same way. I doubt they would blood massacre to express it, however. Yankees would have wreaked their vengeance not with fire but with frost. But I was coming to realize that MHT was hated not for his busybody role as government agent or even as manipulating state senator. He had done something else. He had transgressed four inviolate taboos: he had owned too much of their land, he had married one of their women, he had mocked their codes of honor, and he had threatened to educate their slaves. That's why he had to be removed. And that's why it had to be so violent.

Those taboos were still in place, although the marrying part is hardly taken seriously. That's why no one was going to be the least bit regretful. No one was going to pull me aside and quietly say, "Sorry about your kinsman. We were just at our wit's end." No, that's because they were *not* at their wit's end. They had their wits about them. They made their peace with violence in the service of a worldview that still features land, honor, and race. What happened in the 1870s was not spontaneous violence. It was fully premeditated. A bumper sticker at the Piggly Wiggly explained: "My soldier defends freedom for your honor student." Fighting doesn't have to make sense; it has to feel right, and nothing feels as righteous as fighting for freedom. And the key, of course, is that freedom is notoriously undefined. That is, I think, precisely what the Coushattans after Colfax were thinking. They just wanted their freedom back, even if it meant taking it from someone else.

So I decided again to bide my time before crossing over. We left U.S. 84 and headed up toward Sparta, the town where MHT had first started his career in the Freedmen's Bureau. Then we would go over to Ruston, where my father had given some of MHT's papers to the Louisiana Tech University library, and then back down to camp at Lake Bistineau, a bayou MHT had contracted to help clear of debris in order to open up the Red River.

I could have saved my time. Sparta doesn't exist. At the turn of the century it was literally dismantled by a neighboring town called Arcadia. The Louisiana & Northwest Railroad had bypassed Sparta and gone through Arcadia. The Arcadians came in the night and moved all the town records. They wanted to become the parish seat. There was no negotiation; they just did it. Bullyboy politics. Might makes right. No one complained. All that remains is a black Baptist church established in 1867 in what is called Old (aka black) Sparta. A huge topless oak tree still stands about twenty feet from the front door. That oak, we were told, was used as a hanging tree; that it was right next to the church was not happenstance. That was the point.

Most of the objects held by the Louisiana Tech library I had already seen, although not the full-sized newspaper that MHT started and printed for almost a year. He called it the *Sparta Times*, even though he published it at Starlight Plantation. He rarely mentions this in his *Autobiography*, yet it must have taken time to write and set the type. Why no mention? Was it because in retrospect these words didn't matter? Also at the library, still preserved and in good shape, are the handwritten notes warning him to get out while he still could. Some were from friends and some from foes. It was hard to look at them and realize he had looked at them too. I knew their violent portent; I wondered if, at some level, he did too.

And Lake Bistineau, the swamp I had imagined as the trip bookend of the Okefenokee, was so low that it hardly qualified as a swamp, let alone a lake. It was once the overflow of the Red River when the "raft," or plug, was in place just below Shreveport. Now the defining aspect of this entire countryside was the presence, often just miles apart, of little white pipes poking up from the earth, connecting to small tanks, and then snaking back underground. These were the results of the natural gas boom in the Haynesville Shale, a truly massive field of some 200 trillion feet of natural gas. These tanks were reservoirs that captured the fluids that came up along with the gas. We would see strange tilted trucks that lumbered around to drain these holding tanks. Sometimes we'd see the huge derricks out in the graveled fields. From the road, maybe three hundred yards away, we could hear the drills grinding away through the shale. We stopped at one and just sat listening. We could even hear the hydrofracking pumps roaring. The drillers don't let the gas come straight up the pipe but rather send the deep pipes off at different directions and then inject some chemicals (called "mud") under fierce pressure to bust up the shale formations. The gas is then let loose and comes dutifully to the surface. In the mind-set I was in, even that seemed so spooky, so violent, so deep underground, so far in the muddy past. It was like they were blasting out the Y axis. These lines were converging whether I was ready or not. Maudlin to be sure, but X and Y stories seemed destined to meet.

6

The Red River Valley
What Really Happened

The past is a foreign country: they do things differently there.
—L. P. HARTLEY, *The Go-Between*

We finally retraced our steps to U.S. 84, crossed through the forest like characters in a fairy tale, and made our way to the scene of the family slaughter. Well, not quite to the scene. We made our way to the Grand Bayou RV Park and Resort in Coushatta. The name is rather grand, yet deserved, as it is the nicest place to stay in this parish. Owned by the town and run privately, the campsite is on a man-made expansion of a bayou. My sisters, their companions, and my niece were going to meet us here and stay in a cabin. We'd be in one of the RV slots. Although most RV places we had stayed in were nearly empty—after all, February is not a tourist month in Deep Dixie—this place was more than half full. The major clientele were from Texas, pickup-driving roustabouts who were here drilling for natural gas.

We were going to be shown around Coushatta and the environs by a local historian, Joe Taylor, a retired plant manager for a now shut-down Sunbeam plant. Joe is a history buff and knows just about every step that MHT had taken. That's no mean feat because almost all the action— the massacre and the attempted assassination—took place on the banks of the Red River, and the river has either completely changed course thanks to natural causes, or else been penned in and pushed aside by the irrepressible Army Corp of Engineers.

As with all the big rivers we had seen crossing Dixie (the Flint, the Alabama, the Chattahoochee, the Tombigbee, the Mississippi), the U.S. government was talked into controlling the Red, putting in levees, dams, locks, spillways, and removing all the pretzel twists and backflows that had characterized it generations ago. In MHT's time, in dry spells, boat traffic got held up in Coushatta, unable to make the turn north. Occasionally, you could wade across the river to Starlight Plantation passing grounded steamboats.

No longer. The plantation itself is now deep underwater. Like it or not, the river is of uniform depth all year long. It's been channelized. In one of the unintended consequences of government improvement, no sooner did the river get turned into a barge canal than the railroads cut their shipping rates. Now only a handful of barges make a weekly passage past Coushatta. Bass fishermen are happy; in fact, they are the major beneficiaries. Second in line: RV owners, who can camp out for a pittance on the grounds still managed by the Corp of Engineers. Joe knows this well. He owns an RV that makes mine look like an ice-cream truck.

Colfax

We decided to start our exploration by going south on U.S. 84 to Colfax and working our way back to Coushatta. That way we'd be moving, in a sense, along both the X and Y axes and maybe appreciate better what had happened in the 1870s. I had written to the Red River Heritage Association, and they had put me in touch with a local historian named Avery Hamilton. I had corresponded with Avery, who seemed delightful except that he included a Bible verse with his e-mail signature line. I feared I was going to get an old-style "it was a riot of ungodly blacks" interpretation of what happened in Colfax.

I mentioned to Joe that we were going first to Colfax and invited him along. He said he didn't know much about what had happened in Colfax, which surprised me because the events along the river seemed so connected. Sparks from Colfax lit the tinder in Coushatta. But I was to find out later that this oversight was not strange. Much of local Louisiana history is not known from parish to parish. For instance, in Colfax no one I talked to had heard of the Coushatta massacre.

I don't know what to make of this selective knowledge other than that northern Louisiana is tribal. Family history is really deep, parish history (as counties are called) is deep, regional history is adequate, but what-happened-over-the-hill is shallow. In addition, northern Louisiana doesn't pay much attention to southern Louisiana. And vice versa. This is more than the two Californias or the two Floridas. The southern state is self-consciously French and Spanish, creole, mulatto . . . and cosmopolitan, while the northern is still frontier, sometimes gleefully redneck, and proudly provincial. If north Florida is culturally south Georgia, then north Louisiana is really east Texas. I got the feeling the two Louisianas enjoy not getting along. Maybe this explains the helter-skelter politics and maybe a bit of the shoving matches.

On the way down to Colfax, Joe explained to us how to read the countryside: if you saw a patch of jonquils or daffodils out in a field that usually meant that a house had once been there; a ramshackle double-pen shack could have been a converted slave cabin; a small barn with a little hooded roof was an old commissary where sugar, flour, coffee, and shoes were sold to plantation workers. Joe could tell at a half mile if that little church out in the distance was black Baptist or white.

This part of the Red River valley was rolling land, not flat enough to be profitable for large-scale farming of cotton, rice, or sugar, so it didn't have a real slave population. Prior to the 1830s, the river was too unstable to be used for transportation and hence you couldn't get the crops to market. The land was opened up after the Civil War when the "raft"— the massive logjam—in the river was removed by snag boats and plenty of a new invention, dynamite.

So the glory days of a place like Colfax were between 1860 and 1920, when the river was deep enough for navigation and long enough to carry produce between Shreveport and New Orleans. Driving through the town now you could see the vestiges of palmier days, the stately old hotel, the grand bank with columns, a few big Victorian houses. But those days were short-lived. The tractor ushered in large-scale farming and Walmart ushered out downtown business. And, as we were first aware in Jena, once the white/black ratios moved away from 60/40, the tipping point was crossed. Over the last generation, the ratios in Colfax have flipped. Colfax has turned *bad.*

It was a fitting reminder of my own racism to discover that Avery Hamilton was black. And fitting that in no way was he about to give the *riot* version of history. For him it was pure *massacre.* Avery is a jovial man, a big man with an open face and quick humor. He reminded me of Godfrey Cambridge, the stand-up comedian of the late 1960s. So when he's recalling the grisly details of what happened to his own family it's a bit of a shock; nothing funny about it. Avery's dad is the minister of a nearby church, and Avery is his assistant. For a while Avery sought his fortune in Dallas, but he wanted to come home, back to the land. He married a woman from New Jersey, and, as he said, she still hasn't gotten over what he's gotten her into.

We met Avery outside the library, a strange-looking cement bunker of a building next to the courthouse. He spends a lot of time in the library. He's an amateur genealogist plus local historian. One of his complaints is that it is hard to trace your family tree if you're black. He also spends time looking at records in the courthouse. This is the third Colfax courthouse built on roughly the same place as the one that burned or, more accurately, was burned in 1873. Right out front is the infamous sign announcing that here "marked the end of carpetbag misrule in the South." Avery spends a lot of time in this building too, although he says he's not always welcome. But he wants the sign to stay. It's become a famous reminder of the power of language and storytelling—in this case not to tell the truth, but to obscure the truth.

In front of this courthouse around the sign is a patch of hard-packed earth—all brown, no grass. Supposedly, grass won't grow because it was cursed by the blood of the blacks who were killed there. Years ago, people say, there was a spring here, bubbling up not just water but natural gas. The gas was lit on fire. It made quite a sight and people came by to see it, flames inside water. But the fire has gone out, the spring dried up. Later, in the library, while we were talking to Avery and Doris Lively, the librarian, an old black man, with a string tied around his goatee, assured us that this was all true. Nothing grows until those buried bones are taken care of, he said.

Avery smiles while this is being told. He's heard it before. It's clear

Avery is a thorn in the side of the establishment, both black and white. He enjoys a good dustup. In fact, he's sending his daughter to a private school because he's so upset with the way the public schools are run. New schools are being built, he says, in such a way as to encourage segregation. Why not build one good school and have all the kids attend instead of building new schools in such a way that the blacks inherit the old ones while the whites enjoy the new?

Avery is passionate about education. It's the only way out of this mess. He remembers what happened to him. He was in one of the first integrated classes back in the 1970s. He said that when the teacher called the roll in second grade, she would call out the names of the whites first. Then she would say, "And now the niggers." He said that only then did he begin to realize what his supposed place was. Not only would he have to wait to be counted; he would forever be in the group that comes second. He went home and told his parents. The teacher didn't make it through the semester. He smiles slyly.

Avery knows the power of education, and that is why he wants the truth told about Colfax. Not that grass won't grow over the cursed spot but that no progress will happen until the truth is known. He said that when Charles Lane came to talk about his book, *The Day Freedom Died: The Colfax Massacre, the Supreme Court, and the Betrayal of Reconstruction*, only a handful of white people showed up, and even then there was no real give-and-take, just a polite hearing and then a return to the versions "they came in with." He said blacks didn't come, maybe because many were ashamed. Avery was also disappointed that Lalita Tademy, who wrote a novelization of the incident called *Red River*, didn't come to town to talk to anyone about what happened to the blacks on that Easter Sunday. Blacks need to know their history.

Avery knows the importance of storytelling. Probably the most noteworthy retelling of the Colfax story happened in 2003, when the *Atlantic Monthly* published an article by Richard Rubin called "The Colfax Riot: Stumbling on a Forgotten Reconstruction Tragedy" (July/August). Rubin's point is that stories that don't get told essentially means that events don't happen. As Avery agrees, in many ways *not* telling a story is a more powerful control than telling it wrong.

That's why Avery takes time to show people around town and why he's trying to raise money to start a historical exhibit in the old bank. His last best hope is that Joseph Dorman, a documentary filmmaker at Riverside Films in New York, will see fit to tell the story. Dorman is a winner of television's prestigious George Foster Peabody Award and has been twice nominated for Emmy awards for outstanding cultural and public affairs programming. He says he's interested, but nothing has happened.

What interested me in my own selfish way was that Avery, for all his wanting to get *his* story told, was ignorant of *my* story. He didn't know what happened to my people a few years after the massacre of his. Maybe the stories we really want told are those about how our ox got gored, about what happened to us. What Avery said about cherished stories was true, nonetheless. People will fight harder for a good story than for the truth. A good story makes you feel better, not always the case of the truth.

Later in the week we spent a night at the RV park down by the river near Colfax, a beautiful park, part of the legacy of the billions of dollars spent turning the river into an almost empty barge canal. I asked the park rangers what they knew of the massacre. Both were white middle-aged men, and both were convinced of the truth of their version. One man said the blacks were offered safe passage out of the courthouse if they would surrender, and when they stupidly refused they got what they deserved. And the other said that the blacks had defiled a white minister's dead baby by heaving it out of a coffin. Neither man knew a thing about what happened to the almost fifty blacks who had surrendered, how they had been beaten, stabbed, brutalized, and killed in cold blood. White atrocities didn't fit their stories. They were dubious when I told them that what happened in their little town was the bloodiest single instance of antiblack violence in all U.S. history.

But why should I be surprised that these citizens should not have known their history? Even historians repeated the profane lie until it became . . . received history. That's what makes the historical marker out in front of the courthouse so important a travesty. Here, for instance, are the WPA writers in the late 1930s reporting on what happened: "Here [in Colfax] on Easter Sunday, April 4, 1873, occurred the bloodiest riot of the Reconstruction Period in Louisiana. Under the leadership of a Negro named Ward, Negroes forcibly ejected white municipal and parish officers, and the townspeople fled from their homes. After several days, with the aid of citizens from adjoining parishes, the elected sheriff succeeded in driving out the Negroes, but only after a bloody siege. Three white men and about 120 Negroes were killed" (*Louisiana: A Guide to the State* [Hastings House, 1941]). How easily the words *riot, forcibly ejected, townspeople fled, elected sheriff succeeded, aid of citizens,* and *bloody siege* direct our interpretation.

Down Route 8 south of town is the riverboat cannon used in the siege. It sits in Ben Littlepage's front yard protected on all sides by metal pipes driven into the ground. Mr. Littlepage is one of the wealthiest men in town and a major force in the Louisiana pecan industry. He runs the yearly pecan festival. His shelling and packaging plant is right there on his plantation, and the reason the cannon is surrounded by the pipes is not to protect the cannon from vandalism so much as to make sure the trucks don't run over it while coming in to pick up or leave the pecans. Mr. Littlepage supposedly bought the cannon for the town, but he hasn't been reimbursed, so it's just there for safekeeping.

The cannon looks almost like a child's toy, not at all like what you might see at Vicksburg—more like something from a Boy Scout jamboree. When I called Mr. Littlepage to ask for permission to see the famous ordnance, he said, well, just drive in my driveway and help yourself. He

Riverboat cannon, a so-called 5-pounder, that was used in the Colfax massacre, now in Ben Littlepage's front yard
Photo by Mary Twitchell

was very kind and told his foreman, Sam Daniels, to show us around. So we got the grand tour of not just the cannon but the pecan plant and the slave cabins that Mr. Littlepage has preserved. The two cabins, called *double-pen* because two families shared a common chimney, date from the old Calhoun Plantation days.

Before the Civil War, Meredith Calhoun was one of the largest slave owners and cotton planters in the South, and his slave quarters were built to last. Supposedly, Mr. Calhoun was the template for Simon Legree. He was certainly one of the richest men in North America. His hunchbacked son, William Smith Calhoun, always called Willie, got out of the slave business and fought for emancipation. Willie gave the name Colfax to the town, previously called Calhoun's Landing, as a tribute to Grant's vice president, Schuyler Colfax. And he split the entire parish off from Winn and Rapides, calling it Grant Parish after another president. Willie sided with the blacks in Colfax before the massacre. After the killings, however, he made himself scarce.

I mention this also because Willie is buried in the Colfax town cemetery about a hundred feet from the stone tribute to the men who led the massacre. Here's what their triumphant marble obelisk, a dozen feet high, towering over every other markers, says, all in caps:

IN LOVING REMEMBRANCE
ERECTED TO THE MEMORY OF
THE HEROES,
STEPHEN DECATUR PARISH,
JAMES WEST HADNOT,
SIDNEY HARRIS,
WHO FELL IN THE COLFAX
RIOT FIGHTING FOR
WHITE SUPREMACY
APRIL 13, 1873

It's more than a marker. Like the sign in front of the courthouse, it's a taunt, spit in your eye. Nearby, Willie has a small, scuffed headstone. Scalawag Willie may have had the power to name but not the power to be memorialized.

Obelisk memorializing the fallen heroes "fighting for white supremacy," erected in 1921 by the town fathers of Grant Parish. This not-so-subtle tower is just yards away from a small headstone for Willie Calhoun, the real hero of the piece.
Photo by author

As we were driving back to Coushatta I couldn't help but marvel at the powers of story selection. Mostof the white participants, and their descendants, in this ethnic cleansing have resolutely refused to countenance the truth. And in this case, we know the truth.

The courts knew the truth too. A total of ninety-seven whites were indicted for the killings. Twice, J. R. Beckwith, the U.S. attorney in New Orleans, presented juries with evidence that showed clear violations of the U.S. Enforcement Act of 1870, an offshoot of the Fourteenth Amendment providing protection for blacks. The court in New Orleans had reams of eyewitness reports of the slaughter of the prisoners. Perhaps because the testimony was from blacks, it couldn't be believed. But President Grant had ordered troops to restore order to Colfax, and 2d Lt. George D. Wallace, acting assistant adjutant-general, District of Upper Red River, had submitted his report confirming what the eyewitnesses saw. Because the bodies of those tortured and maimed were not buried, they were there for all to see.

The first trial (1874) ended with an acquittal for one killer and a mistrial for all the others. In the retrial there were three convictions, which were appealed and overturned when the Enforcement Act was essentially ruled unenforceable. Ultimately the Supreme Court decided that the individual states, not the United States, should deal with these matters.

Forget the judicial system and technicalities. The not-so-simple fact of the matter is that although enough evidence was there to prove that this had been a brutal massacre of black prisoners, neither side wanted to hear this story. One of the points that Lalita Tademy makes in her introduction to her novelization *Red River* is that many survivors—some of her kinfolk—were so traumatized that they wouldn't tell what had happened, even to their families. Their black versions stayed put, traveling down through generations in whispers.

But what about the whites? Why didn't they brag about their exploits? After all, they could claim they had put down this *riot* with such panache and dispatch. Setting the courthouse afire was such a clever move, and using the cannon to shoot the blacks inside their own embankments was inspired. Plus, they only lost three men (one—James Hadnot—seems to have been accidentally shot by his own men because the bullet holes were all in his back).

Were the whites mum because of shame? Were they ashamed that the black prisoners were ridden like cows and then kicked and knifed to death, were they ashamed that youngsters were allowed to put a gun to the heads of two Negroes side by side and then see if a bullet would go through both, were they ashamed that they had ridden on horseback behind the smoke-asphyxiated prisoners and shot them down like dogs from behind, were they ashamed that they haphazardly dumped the bodies of the dead on the banks of the river, hoping that they would float away?

No, I don't think so. No more so than the Germans, Japanese, Argentineans, Guatemalans, Rwandans, Somalians, Sri Lankans . . . were shamed by their acts. What happened in Colfax is something quite common in human history, the activity of a self-appointed death squad, of humans *not* gone berserk but behaving rationally. Shame is involved all right, but not shame of the act. Humans act like this when they have been so shamed by other acts that this is what they do, ironically, to become free of shame. The blacks were scapegoats, and killing them was the way out of shameland. The whites had lost *face*, now they were getting it back by literally destroying black faces.

Here's the key, I think. The White League wasn't silent from fear that they would get caught and punished. Not at all. In *United States v. Cruikshank* (1876), the Supreme Court essentially gave them a get-out-of-jail pass. The State of Louisiana did not, and was not going to, prosecute any of the killers. So self-incrimination was not the motivation for quietude.

I think the murderers kept quiet about their acts because, while they knew slaughter violated their vaunted code of honor and chivalric principles, they also knew—or believed—it was the only way for them to survive. They could say that the blacks were subhuman and deserved to be put down, but that doesn't explain the method of putting down. Even lynching, their usual recourse, has the illusion of due process. In fact, hangings were often called "the sentence of Judge Lynch," as if the act were not entirely capricious.

But I didn't really appreciate that conundrum until I began to think about what had happened a few months after Colfax in Coushatta. And oddly enough, it was my great-grandfather's *Autobiography* that helped me understand what men do when they feel they can do nothing. Hopelessness is sometimes an empowering way to feel. Why not act? What's to lose?

Coushatta

In his autobiography, *Carpetbagger from Vermont: The Autobiography of Marshall Harvey Twitchell* (1989), my great-grandfather is forever going on about this thing he calls *the chivalry*. He always uses the word with the definite article, not as "the chivalric code" or "members of the chivalry," but simply "*the* chivalry." It took me some time to figure out what he was doing. While he does have a self-deprecating sense of humor (especially about his exploits as a young man in the Civil War), I wasn't expecting sarcasm, especially not about southern honor. But when he talks about his experiences in trusting southerners, in understanding their code, he is almost always mocking. It's one of the reasons I think that he and his family were attacked. Mocking honor is inviting disaster.

For instance, here he is on the subject of courtship honor. When his fiancée (Adele Coleman) pulls out his gun and shoots at a rejected suitor who has been harassing her, MHT observes: "I have since learned enough of the customs and ideas of the Southern people to know that had she hit the young man, it would have been pronounced an accident. He, a young man of one of the first families, could not have been so dishonorable as to have been eavesdropping, while she could not have intentionally shot him. A certain pride and honor were of more importance than life to them." Or, of his thoughts that the White League might be massing for an attack on Coushatta after the massacre at Colfax, he writes: "The white Republican leaders, with horses and arms, were to remain at Coushatta. In a few hours the parish was thoroughly alarmed and the chivalry, feeling confident that they would have something to do besides shooting unarmed negroes, abandoned the project." Or, in 1873, after the Colfax massacre, he predicted that there would be a shortage of corn. He hedged by buying as much seed corn as he could afford. True to his prediction, there was a dearth of seed. Here's what he did: "I instructed my agent to give each man but one load of corn, to take no mortgage or any other security for it, charge it to the receiver, and leave it to his honor about payment. This was an unheard of procedure to them and resulted in a complete capture of the affections of the people that they declared themselves supporters of mine. . . . I adopted this liberal method of dealing with them, not for political purposes, but because, from my study of Southern character, I had discovered that they would readily pay a debt of honor and let the secured debt go unpaid." After Colfax, as the White League starts lynching blacks in Coushatta, MHT comments: "Two colored men were arrested and hung on a tree just at the edge of town, serving as amusement for the chivalry and an excuse for keeping together their military force."

On the slaughter of his family in the Coushatta massacre, he bitterly says: "The whole story is for the chivalry one of treachery, cowardice, and dishonor. The prisoners submitted to arrest upon the assurance of the Democratic leaders that it would allay the excitement, prevent the murder of negroes, and protect from harm the women and children belonging to them. They were kept disarmed so that they could offer no dangerous resistance to their own murder and robbery, to the brave and honorable chivalry that, according to their own statement, never strikes a fallen foe." And only now does the mask of irony drop: "As a matter of fact the so-called Southern chivalry is a remnant of the dark ages which they copy, and although they have some desirable qualities, they also have many of the savage and barbarous characteristics of the lower civilization to which they belong." At first I thought this sarcasm was just his superciliousness, his Yankee hauteur, his—let's face it—cloying self-righteousness. But the more I thought about it, the more I realized that he had isolated a core of Dixie culture: the obsession with honor, point zero of the Y axis. As my colleague Bertram Wyatt-Brown has argued in his magisterial *Southern Honor: Ethics and Behavior in the Old South*, obsessions with protecting bloodlines, slavery, and land may raise the ire, but honor pulls the trigger. It's why there was the dueling sandbar north of Natchez, why lynching occurred with such frequency (almost always to defend a woman's honor), why such hopeless displays of courage as Pickett's charge were valorized, why honorable defeat (the noble but hopeless cause) becomes so central to the pulsing heart of Dixie. The "South will rise again" is not so much a call to arms as it is a balm to temporize dishonor.

This is still why, I think, that when you ask many southerners for the cause of the war, they are unwilling to mention slavery. No, they say, it was not about slavery; it was about states' rights, freedom to choose, the restoration of home rule, heroic individualism. There's nothing honorable about slavery, but everything honorable about protecting freedom of choice. Honor is not what you do (enslavement of another person) but how you appear in the eyes of others (protecting rights).

Honor, Shame, and Religion

Honor has a nasty corollary: shame. Shame is not what you do, but how you appear in the eyes of others. Guilt is different. Guilt is how you appear to yourself. You feel guilty; other people shame you. Honor cultures are especially susceptible to shame. Such cultures tend to be sealed off, island cultures, with a rigid social hierarchy. Think Japan. Stay in line.

Follow rules. Or you'll be shamed. Shame in such cultures is a buried electric fence that keeps certain behaviors at arm's length by severely jolting the trespasser.

All cultures use shame. Today we shame cigarette smokers, child molesters, fat people, people who use the N-word, RV owners. But the electric fence moves around. When I was a kid, shame was invoked for people who used vulgar language in front of women, got divorced, filed for bankruptcy, didn't salute the flag, and you know the rest.

What I think happened in the Red River area during Reconstruction is that shame became simply overwhelming for the males. Social codes had snapped. Bad enough to lose the war, worse that Yankees were delegating the day-to-day decisions, and intolerable that blacks were not just equals but, in a sense, superiors, at least at the ballot box. Slaves were not just freed; they were in power. When this kind of shaming happens, almost any action is preferable, even mass suicide . . . or mass slaughter. The illusion of propriety is given up not to anarchy but to restoration of lost order. To appease group shame, death squads often are formed. That's because really brutal behavior is so powerful an act that it momentarily stops the agony of shame.

Often this carnage is directed against a scapegoat, literally an animal slaughtered for the release of the group pressure. In ancient days the palliative scapegoat supposedly was a goat driven off into the wilderness. For the Jews this happened on Yom Kippur, the Day of Atonement. For the rite to work properly, the totemic animal carries away the sin; its spilled blood washes us clean.

In this context, one can see why anthropologists like René Girard (*Violence and the Sacred*) make this resolution of trauma part of an explanation of the attraction of literalist Christianity. Kill the Christ, who dies for our sins; then mourn the act and repent. Could this be why the Baptist religion, which is so drenched in the blood of Christ, is the dominant religion for much of southern culture? And why it's so pugnacious in its fundamentalism that it will brook no metaphoric readings?

There is a famous and not entirely unfair blasphemy of American Protestantism that goes like this: A Baptist is a Christian who has learned to wash; a Methodist is a Baptist who has learned to read; a Presbyterian is a Methodist who has gone to college; and an Episcopalian is a Presbyterian whose investments have turned out well. The Baptist, especially the Southern Baptist, is of the denomination most concerned with getting clean, getting forgiven, getting free of shame. In many respects, the Southern Baptist is the most irrepressible, the most in-your-face believer because he is really confronting sin and degradation in a way other denominations prefer to pass by. Maybe as well it's because he knows he has something quite specific to be ashamed of.

I remember seeing a roadside sign: a large wooden cross with *Blood Redemption Secured* carved across the top. The concept was so sophisticated, the language so erudite, yet the bargain immediately understood. *I must have redemption now and I have got it,* or, *I've dealt with my shame; sorry about yours.* The statement is aggressive, yes, it's almost a call to action. Being washed in the blood of Christ, being baptized, drains off the shame, lessens the confusion of an anxious life, and makes civil interaction possible. The irony is almost insupportable; the killing of Jesus becomes the violent act that stops the shame of believers. That we now atone for this act in no way makes it less powerful; it only shows how base we are and how forgiving the Redeemer is. Acknowledging sin may feel bad, but it's really a way around worse feelings, around feeling dreadful shame.

The key is that shame confronted head-on often leads to violence. And the Deep South, the Old South, has learned this. I realize that this sounds like something from someone who is paid to make simple things complicated, but the question of why the Southern Baptist religion, so obsessed with blood, is the oligopoly religion across all the Deep South almost invites this kind of interpretation. It has become the religion for these people because it resolves the particular problem of these people and the "peculiar institution" they adopted. *Redemption now!* lifts them over the furious backwash of enslaving other human beings. It circumvents anxiety and retrospection with the promise of almost immediate gratification. "I've sinned. I'm reborn. I'm saved." As the signs all over the inside of the Salem Heights Baptist Church, located on Glory Hill outside Laurel, Mississippi, said, "You Must Be Born Again."

This role of Jesus as *personal* savior also may help explain why the

Jews, the favorite scapegoat for much of the rest of the Western world, were given a free pass south of the Mason-Dixon line. As we saw, Jews were all through the little towns of Deep Dixie. And they were not just tolerated but often invited. True, they traded with the blacks and thus were a crucial link in the financial chain, and, true, they were also willing to dirty themselves with downtown trade, but the southern gentry and yeomen didn't stigmatize them, as did the North. The South had other scapegoats. Cue the carpetbaggers. Southern Baptists still support many Jewish causes, like the state of Israel (often because of Apocalyptic expectations), but I wonder if the roots of this sympathy go back into the nineteenth century.

One of the most interesting characters in the story of the rise and fall of MHT was a Jewish merchant, Joseph Lisso. The Lissos came from eastern Europe, migrated to New Orleans, and then two of the Lisso brothers came up to Coushatta to open a hardware store. When MHT separated Red River Parish from the surrounding parishes and started developing Coushatta as a trading center, no family was more helpful than the Lissos. But as the tide turned and things started to run against the Vermonters (doubtless a function of the nepotism, taxation, and the financial depression), the Lissos shifted allegiances; by the time of the massacre, they had cast their lot with the White League.

With carpetbaggers gone by the 1880s, the Jews started to play their traditional scapegoat role. In the 1960s, the southern anger was often directed at the northern Jews who, sympathetic with the plight of the blacks, came South to register voters and support such alphabet groups as the NAACP, SNCC, and SCLC. And it was often those Jews, the so-called New York Jews, who now played the role of the intrusive outsider, stirring things up. Supposedly, they controlled (and still control) the media—conveniently not Fox News, however.

Baptists were concerned. In 1972, when Rev. Billy Graham was confiding in President Nixon that Jews had too much power and that "they swarm around me and are friendly to me, because they know that I am friendly to Israel and so forth, but they don't know how I really feel about what they're doing to this country, and I have no power and no way to handle them," these are some of the Jews he's referring to. Nixon replies: "You must not let them know" (Watergate tapes, February 1, 1972).

Certainly the two most famous of these Jews in the South were Andrew Goodman and Michael Schwerner, who, along with James Chaney, a black man, were brutally killed in June 1964 in Neshoba County just north of where U.S. 84 goes through Laurel, Mississippi. They had come south to register black voters and were going to look at a recently torched church. The parallels with the Coushatta massacre are eerie. The Yankee intruders were jailed on trumped-up charges, released after dark, and then, supposedly granted safe passage out of town, were led into a trap of KKK killers, who did the deed. Their bodies were then sloppily bulldozed into an earthen dam.

Their disappearance was national news. When the FBI finally located the bodies, as well as the bodies of others—all blacks—the State of Mississippi refused to prosecute for murder even though they knew the identity of the killers. So, as with Colfax and Coushatta, the U.S. Justice Department stepped in, charging some of the killers with conspiring to deprive the three of their civil rights (by murder). This time, however, the U.S. government stood firm. The charges were lodged against the sheriff, deputy sheriff, and sixteen others. The case dragged on, becoming more important as a book and movie—*Mississippi Burning*—than as an example of expeditious justice. Finally in 2005, almost a half century later, justice was feebly served when the last of the killers was indicted on three counts of murder. He was prosecuted and convicted by the state; he appealed the verdict, which was confirmed in 2007. This was a century and a quarter after Colfax.

Coushatta Today

I mention this conjunction between shame/violence/scapegoating because of several events that happened in Coushatta in 2009 that made me think of the 1870s. First, at a dinner party given by Joe Taylor, one of his guests, a distinguished lawyer and local politician, said that of course MHT was hated and here's why. He said that when MHT wanted to buy land, he looked for the weakest landowner, almost always a Confederate widow, had her taxes raised, and then when she couldn't pay, he bought her land at foreclosure prices. The next day we met another elderly Coushattan who said the same thing almost word for word: MHT bought land from Confederate widows whose taxes he had purposefully raised to confiscatory levels. If there was one thing I had learned on U.S. 84, it is that in the Deep South land is blood.

Now I have no doubt that MHT bought land from Confederate widows, but his primary holdings were bought from the Gillespie family, for which he paid what looks to be a fair market price—twenty-one thousand dollars for Starlight Plantation. No scholars who have dealt with MHT have said a word about this fleecing of Confederate widows.

This comment has the smack of Victorian melodrama. The nasty banker polishing the wax mustache, tying the damsel to the train tracks, and buying land from the poor widow is a powerful trope. A more probable reason (and one I rarely heard mentioned) why MHT was despised was far more obvious, but a bit more difficult to admit. He wanted to enfranchise and educate the blacks. In fact, he was adamant about it. That had been his job. True, he became a state senator, and true, he ran what was essentially a political ring. But he knew education of blacks was the only way out of this mess. He built schools on his own property. His sister taught in the black school. He assured the locals that if they burned down the black school, he would do the same for the white, and, worse, he did indeed tax the populace for schools for both races. The tax rates for Coushatta were not markedly different from those in surrounding parishes. I suspect that teaching the blacks to read, write, and vote was the third rail, not the exploiting of Confederate widows. But nothing trumps the image of the rapacious Yankee turning out the frail widow from what remains of her few family acres. If only he could be doing it in a driving snowstorm.

And the other comment I heard was from Jimmy Marston III. Jimmy is my counterpart in this morality play as he is the great-grandson of Bulow Marston, one of the men who played a part in the killing of the Twitchell clan as well as perhaps being a co-conspirator in the assassination attempt of MHT. Jimmy said on the phone when I first talked to him that as a child the name Twitchell was a moniker used to strike terror into hearts of children, by which I think he meant white children.

In the 2003 PBS show *Reconstruction: The Second Civil War,* Jimmy discusses the assassination attempt:

NARRATOR: The assassin's identity was never revealed.

MARSTON: There's some speculation as to, uh, it being my great-grand-father. He was the kind of man that could have done it. If it had to be done, he would have done it.

NARRATOR: Amazingly, Twitchell survived the shooting. He was taken to a house a few miles from Coushatta, where both his arms were amputated.

READING [from *Autobiography*], MARSHALL TWITCHELL: I turned my face to the window, watching the sun as it disappeared behind the trees, reviewing my past life, and trying to imagine what would be my future in the world.

NARRATOR: A delegation of local black ministers came to pay their respects.

TUNNELL [Twitchell biographer]: The concern of these ministers was not simply for Twitchell himself, but for all he represented. He represented this dream of a truly biracial society in which black people would be treated with respect and dignity. And he's almost a corpse now, and he becomes a metaphor for their own broken dreams.

NARRATOR: The White League in Coushatta had a very different reaction. "Our people rejoiced at it," B. W. Marston recalled, "as much as they would at the killing of any tyrant in the world."

MARSTON: Everyone was very happy that Twitchell was gone. We're still happy today that he's gone. (www.pbs.org/wgbh/amex/reconstruction/filmmore/pt_p2.html)

If I get his point correctly, my great-grandfather was somehow responsible for the tribulations experienced in northern Louisiana, tribulations still being experienced. Everyone was happy? Including blacks? I realize I'm not a disinterested observer of these characterizations, but two comments:

1. If MHT were such a tyrant, why is there no hint of this in his life before he became head of the Freedmen's Bureau and no hint of

it after he left Coushatta? Before Coushatta, he was universally praised for his courage and soldierly skills, and after Coushatta, as head of the consular office in Kingston, Canada, he was praised for his diplomatic skills, generosity, and kindness. How come he was a tyrant only in Coushatta?

2. Blaming MHT for destabilizing this section of the South is fair, but demonizing him seems extreme. He was only in Louisiana for a bit more than ten years, from 1865 to 1877. Was he so virulent that his influence lasted for more than a hundred years? Or was the *resurrection* of antebellum culture responsible for the plight of the Deep South? Any possibility that, to paraphrase Pogo, we have met the tyrant and he is us? No one questions that Reconstruction was an awkward failure, but was that because it was conceptually flawed or never really fully applied?

But this self-serving caviling is beside the point. Nothing trumps a good story. And almost no story is better than the tyrant exploiting elderly widows in his lust for land. The story doesn't just establish southern victimization, it begs redress. It's a version of what was behind the Coushatta massacre, namely, a story that men, in this case the blacks, are after our women. Women are so weak. Only the chivalry can protect them.

Once we were in Coushatta, and once it was clear that our only interest was family curiosity (and not claiming rights to any property atop the Haynesville Shale or contradicting the received story), we could all move on. In fact, we Twitchells could see in the white version of the story not only the plight of these southerners but also MHT's obliviousness to that plight. The Old South was in dire shape in the 1870s. No doubt about it. That's why these stories were so important and, to some degree, why they still are.

The True Story

We had been telling ourselves stories too. Joe Taylor and Jimmy Marston put us straight. According to both local historians, the story that we and PBS had been told that the murders of the Twitchell clan were done by the mysterious Texans was a fraud. The creation of lone wolf Captain Jack was a fraud. The assassination attempt was real enough, but the shooter wasn't this Captain Jack. The story had been concocted by the townsmen of Coushatta, fed to the newspapers (most importantly to M. L. Pickens, editor of the Republican *Coushatta Times*, who printed it September 5, 1874, as well as to Mary Bryan, the author of *Wild Work* (see www.rootsweb.ancestry.com/~laredriv/coushatta_times .htm), and—this is the amazing part—the story was never contradicted. At least never in public.

I've never been in a group of more than four people where a secret can be kept for longer than a month. Of course, academic groups are notoriously gossipy. But here was a secret kept by more than a handful of men and kept for generations. The men involved swore an oath of secrecy and they meant it. What needs to be kept in mind is that everyone, save a few Yankees, was advantaged by keeping the secret: the town, the state, the nation, to say nothing of the murderers themselves. They kept it so well that even the historians of the WPA told the story their way (white suppression of black uprising) in the 1930s. Here's what the Louisiana WPA guide says: "The Coushatta riots occurred here in 1874, when a unit of the White League, supported by men of Red River and adjoining parishes, quelled an uprising of Negroes. The Negroes, led by unscrupulous carpetbaggers, had threatened to exterminate all native white people in the community."

Threatened to exterminate all native white people in the community seems a bit over the top of the top. Here's the true story according to both Joe and Jimmy. They did not tell what they knew to Ted Tunnell, author of the biography, nor to the PBS writers, because they weren't sure how their stories were going to play out. Plus, as Jimmy says, they were never asked.

After the war the Deep South—the land I had been driving across— was a miserable place. No place more miserable than northern Louisiana. Men came home beaten up and maimed, having lost most of their companions, deeply shamed by defeat. In Red River Parish, the blacks outnumbered the whites by about four to one. For a while (until 1868) some vets couldn't vote without signing an oath. They had no money, literally. There was no currency but the Union dollar. Plantation script was worthless. If Louisiana had had more millionaires before the war than any other state, now it had more penniless derelicts. Desolation barely defines it.

Now here comes this Yankee, MHT, who marries a southern girl (a breach of her family's honor, to be sure), buys a plantation, threatens to buy more, employs blacks at high wages, makes a profit, gets the blacks to help elect him to the senate, pleases prominent whites by making a new parish, and then starts to import his kin to do his dirty work: levy taxes, decide who votes, set the wage structure, arbitrate disputes. He works to educate and enfranchise blacks and provide them security and justice. This does not go unnoticed. His detractors grow. Whenever he gets into a tight spot, all he has to do is call for troops and the blue coats appear.

So the Coushattans do what they had done in the war. They form command lines to insulate themselves from counterattack and plan for the eventual eviction of the foreigners and the *Resurrection*—and that's the word used complete with religious overtones—of the old order. Not only do they have the template of battlefield hierarchy, but most are also members of the Masonic order.

It's hard to overestimate the importance of the Masons in the nineteenth century. They were, in both North and South, the social filament that held men into a predictable order, even when that order was contradicted by the demands of politics. There are numerous examples of Masonic soldiers looking out for each other, even when they were on the opposite sides in battle. Once one of them issues the distress call, "Will no one help the widow's son?" other Masons are honor-bound to help. MHT even had his life saved because he gave the Masonic entreaty after being wounded at Wilderness. And two of the members of the Twitchell ring (Henry A. Scott and George King) were possibly saved from the Coushatta massacre because they were Masons.

The plan to dispatch the Twitchell ring, hatched over months and put into place after Colfax, was to capture all the carpetbaggers, MHT included, and then go through the ritual of giving them safe passage out of the state. A similar, almost simultaneous, purge of Republicans occurred in nearby Natchitoches, but no Republicans were killed. En route would be the massacre—or maybe just the threat of one, it's not clear—and the

Coushattans would testify that the attack came from the west, by Texans led by the mysterious Captain Jack. What messed up this plan was the commotion at Homer Twitchell's house on August 27, 1874. A White League picket was shot by a black man. The picket rode back into town, less than a mile, alerting the townspeople that a black rebellion was in the offing.

The plan of rounding up the Yankees, along with some blacks, was put into gear, perhaps prematurely. That they didn't also pick up MHT in the dragnet was unfortunate for them. However, maybe it tamped down the danger of notoriety and made it safer that he was alive in New Orleans. Surely, Senator Twitchell would see in the slaughter of his kin (or even just the threat) that there was no place for him in northern Louisiana. He would, surely, leave.

As we know, he didn't. Just the opposite. After safe passage was promised, the slaughter occurred. Maybe it wasn't intended by everyone involved at the planning stage, maybe things went haywire, but the results were real enough. The killings happened. And the destruction of his family didn't deter MHT, but only toughened his resolve. Ironically, the one thing he did as a result, and it may have been crucial, is that he resigned from the Masons in disgust. His brother Homer had applied for membership three times and three times had been blackballed. Now with Homer dead, MHT's resignation may have severed whatever protective tie he had to the world around him.

But how was he going to be killed? Here both Joe and Jimmy agree. The men who had done the earlier killing met in secret, broke into smaller cells. They had to have plausible deniability should the Feds find out. Remember, there was a small posting of Union soldiers still in Coushatta after the massacre. So the Rebels bided their time. Perhaps Twitchell would wise up and leave. They gave him plenty of time.

And then when he didn't, the leaders of the White League met again in secret. They decided to draw lots and the one with the short stick would be the one to do the deed, take Twitchell out, and the others would close ranks behind him. No one knows how many were in this elite group, probably between three and ten. They agreed that they would use the Captain Jack persona from the earlier massacre to describe the killer. The selected shooter, wearing the disguise, would do the deed and then leave for Texas to return when the dust had settled. There would be no white eyewitnesses; all would leave their places of business and be up near the post office when the shots were fired. Let the blacks report what they saw, so much the better for the terrifying effect on them. The League even seeded the event with mysterious threats from the goggle-eyed man that MHT dutifully saved, such as this one:

> Twitchell Ring, Harrison, and others of the Court House ring I as a friend, I would advise you to leave this part of the country for it has become so (?) Unhealthy that you can't stay here and I, as the google-eyed man would advise you to leave as soon as you can for you cant live here anyway, whatever, for I have been maid to leave my home & friends & family on the account of you and your crowd. Now please take my advice, all of the court house ring, from the wilds of Californy

> The goggle ied man.

> Take this advice on time & leave, the last one of you, for I will come again at the proper time

> Goggle ied man

So they waited until they knew MHT would be back from New Orleans, coming into town for a meeting of what is still called the police jury, a town commissioner meeting. MHT was to be shot on the town side of the river in full view of the Negroes; then the disguised shooter would ride up the river, change clothes, and head out across the state line to Texas and safety. Money had been raised for his exile, and the local townspeople would care for his family.

All went according to plan. MHT was shot, the shooter headed out of town, the posse was dutifully called together, they followed the trail for a bit more than a mile and then conveniently lost it as the assassin presumably crossed the river. The black eyewitnesses, true to form, reported the overcoat, the slouch hat, the fake beard, and, most importantly, the green goggles. The story was congruent with the earlier massacre and the tellers of the tale were in place, as were the listeners. Better yet, Captain Jack was in place. And he would stay there for generations.

Note to Marshall Harvey Twitchell from the "Goggle-eyed man"
In possession of the author

I heard Joe's version in Coushatta, but I had to go to Shreveport a few days later to hear Jimmy's. From my first correspondence with Jimmy he had hinted that he had information he wanted my family to know. I must admit I was apprehensive since he had appeared on the PBS show saying that MHT was a tyrant deserving of his fate. Jimmy said he had his great-aunt's diary as well as an object that has remained secret for 140 years. He wanted to show them to us.

I had no idea what the secret could be other than that I was preparing myself to meet a long-lost cousin or see some incriminating evidence of MHT's supposed tyranny. So when Jimmy suggested he call the local newspapers so we could do this in public, I shuddered and begged off. We had no idea how we'd feel in Louisiana, let alone feel when presented with some hitherto unknown information and/or object. In truth, my deepest fear was that he would present me with a roomful of mulatto cousins.

We met Jimmy at Joe Taylor's cocktail and dinner party, and he wasn't at all the chauvinistic bullyboy I had seen on the PBS show. In fact, quite the opposite. He is a tall, soft-spoken, good-looking man who has a charming personality, as well he should for his job is a land buyer for a Texas oil company. He grew up in the area, knows all the local people, and is an avid historian. He's one of those Civil War buffs who, if you mention a battle, can tell you not just the names of the commanders but almost all the names of the dead. In spite of myself, I was much taken with him, as was the rest of my family.

So when he promised again to show us something special that he had in Shreveport, we jumped at the invitation and on February 22 went to his home. His assistant, Mildred Worrell, assured us we'd not be disappointed. The evening started rather formally with his showing us all the family portraits, including one of Bulow, hanging in the house. Even a portrait of his teenage son is hanging up there along with Robert E. Lee. Like many southerners, the Marstons take the abstract concept of blood seriously. The family had come south from Massachusetts to settle before the war. If his ancestors didn't sign the Declaration, they should have. A direct ancestor, John Marston, had been one of the Sons of Liberty who dumped the tea during the Boston Tea Party. Once in the South, however, the younger Marstons sided with the Confederacy while the patriarch, Henry Marston (John's son and Jimmy's great-great-grandfather), was not an abolitionist but an antisecessionist. In fact, during the war, Henry proudly flew the Stars and Stripes over his Louisiana home. That brave, albeit foolhardy, act almost cost him his life.

Out came the Marston family treasures, guns, documents, trophies, and memorabilia, even the original deed to Starlight Plantation. I wasn't sure what to make of this relic display other than that I think Jimmy wanted us to know that the roots of his family ran deep and that it was really by happenstance that our great-grandfathers ended up antagonists. Their roles could have been reversed. As my niece later observed, we were all bringing to dinner what our parents had told us. "I'm saying my lies, they're saying theirs," she said.

After dinner, Jimmy made a toast "to Americans." I must say I thought that was rather ominous but I think his point was, enough is enough. Time to furl the flags; it's over. Keep your hard feelings if you want, keep telling your stories, but they don't do anyone any good. He told us the same massacre and assassination version that Joe had related, only this time he cited his great-aunt's diary as the source. As we talked about it, it was so clear that the "Texans did it" was flimsy on the face of it. In the Coushatta massacre it had been prearranged that the safekeeping party would simply stand aside so that the killing group could do its task. Everyone knew that the "protectors" were in cahoots with the "marauders." That's why it happened so efficiently. There was no need for Captain Jack. The promise of safe passage out of Louisiana was a fraud from the get-go.

And in the assassination attempt most of the eyewitnesses were the blacks who could be counted on to be mortified by what they saw and to report the outlandish disguise of the killer. The whites had conveniently all gone over to the post office. In fact, Jimmy said, he had heard that the killer (who was about eighty feet from MHT when taking aim) had sought only to wound him. After all, the marksman had shot the hand of the ferryman and killed George King, the brother-in-law. Surely, such a good shooter could have done the killing had he wanted. Perhaps he had wanted only to maim MHT. But Jimmy thought this was more the stuff of legend than fact. I did too. The point of the assassination attempt, however, was not just to dispatch MHT but also to make sure that everyone knew that the shooter's identity was Captain Jack.

Then, while we were digesting this, Jimmy asked to be excused from the table and left the room. He returned a short time later with a small dark-lacquered eyeglass case, like the kind you would use for reading glasses. He put it down in front of me. "Open it," he said. I did. Inside was a pair of eyeglasses, smallish, with a panel below each temple that folded out so that they gave a wraparound look. They certainly were not goggles such as I had imagined. I had imagined swimming goggles or what was worn while driving a Model T, ones with a leather strap to go around the head. In fact, they looked just like the yellow safety glasses worn by skeet shooters. Only in a shade of darkish green and much smaller. I had seen such glasses earlier in small-town museums.

My wife, at the other end of the table, said, put them on, let's see what they look like on you. And without thinking, I did. I didn't have them on for long, and I must admit it was spooky. They were tight on my temples. Just being close to something I had heard about for years and now actually having them on and seeing not just them, but *through* them, gave me a start. I quickly passed the glasses to my sister.

Jimmy said the glasses had come to his great-grandfather and were then passed down through the family. He found them in a safe-deposit box with the diary and some letters. We were told that on the way out of town the assassin stopped at Jimmy's great-grandfather's plantation to change clothes and left behind his costume and goggles. Jimmy told us the name of the shooter, and we promised not to tell. We had earlier seen his grave. The assassin had not been mentioned in any of the histories. He came back from Texas after the election of Rutherford B. Hayes and the Compromise of 1877, which essentially granted him amnesty. This was the compromise effected by the Republicans and in a sense signed off on by MHT when he returned to New Orleans to cast his vote for Hayes. The Compromise reversed much of MHT's life work but gave him the cushy job in Canada. The irony is just too overwhelming. He must have known it was returning the blacks to servitude, but he couldn't have known it was also giving his assassin safe passage home.

All evening long I kept repeating the assassin's name to myself, the name I had promised not to divulge. I was going to have to remember it so I could tell my grandchildren. They would want to know, and if I didn't remember it, this part of the story would disappear.

That night back in the RV, I woke in a sweat. I had seen the world for a second just as the shooter had. Our eyes had not met, but they had seen light through the same prism. I didn't know who he was, but I knew his name. That was empowering, something to wrap the brain around. And in a way I had also seen my great-grandfather in a slightly different light, as a victim of a culture I had become strangely sympathetic with. For just a moment, a line between X and Y flashed, points had touched.

Homeward Bound

Sometimes it's hard to know when a trip ends, but mine did when I put on those glasses. After all, seeing things from another perspective is one reason to leave home. Or so the travel agents say. And indeed I had done that, almost too literally. I had hoped that when my trip was done I'd be able to see certain things more clearly, have an understanding of what happened in the 1870s, and be able to do what any road-tripper intends, namely, tell a good story about it. Instead I'm not sure I really saw *the* truth, or at least the truth I was after, through those glasses darkly. I got just a glint of understanding, not a real picture.

I wanted a wide-screen, 3-D epiphany, a "silent-upon-a-peak-in-Darien" experience, a brass-band understanding, not just a pop. I wanted to solve for X and solve for Y. I wanted to see a distinct line on the graph—here's how you go from A to B. Here's how it happened. Now you know. No ambiguity, no fuzziness. On the way home I felt a leak of deflation. Did I really understand those massacres? Instead, I began to realize why no one cares much about the return passage. The quest out is full of expectation, the journey back is dreary anticlimax. I was tempted to drop down to Interstate 10, merge into the fast lane, and auto-pilot my way back home and into the bathtub.

This desire to *be done with it* seems true for make-believe travelers as well—Christian in *Pilgrim's Progress*, Don Quixote, Robinson Crusoe, Ishmael, Tom Jones, Lemuel Gulliver, Marlow in *Heart of Darkness*, Frodo in *Lord of the Rings*, even Humbert Humbert—are pooped at the end. They're tripped out. Even if you've found your goal, you still have to get back home. Those old road warriors are either heading for bed, out to the garage for a smoke, or to jail, as the case may be. I came to envy Dorothy. All she had to do to get back to Kansas was to click her heels together three times and say, "There's no place like home," and—whoosh—she's back in her own comfy bed surrounded by loving family. Maybe the really savvy road-tripper is Huck Finn. He's wise enough not to go home: "I reckon I got to light out for the territory ahead of the rest, because Aunt Sally she's going to adopt me and sivilize me, and I can't stand it. I been there before."

Travel writers also experience this homebound malaise. Jack Kerouac,

Herman Melville (*Typee*), V. S. Naipaul, Henry James (*The American Scene*), Theodore Dreiser (*A Hoosier Holiday*), Paul Theroux, Henry Miller (*The Air-Conditioned Nightmare*) are dragging their feet at the end. You never quite get where you want to go. At the end of *Travels with Charley*, Steinbeck says a good journey begins months before you leave home with the maps on the dining room table but ends abruptly a week before you expect it to. In many ways, William Least Heat-Moon gets off the road in the best shape, perhaps because he was in such doldrums at the beginning.

To comfort myself driving eastward, I tried to list all the road films that end in a whimper or a bang—literally. In serious road movies you often don't get home or, if you do, you're in worse shape than when you left. Think *Easy Rider, Into the Wild, Thelma and Louise, About Schmidt, Vanishing Point, Rain Man, Sideways, Stand by Me, La Strada, Larger Than Life, Mad Max, Midnight Run, Paris, Texas, Wild at Heart,* or *Natural Born Killers*. Chances are that a destination-based road trip will net you some serious disappointment.

As you can see, I had a lot of time on the way home to resolve my own lack of perfect solution. I'll spare you my observations about road-trip songs ("Born to Run" by Bruce Springsteen; "Another Travelin' Song" by Bright Eyes; "On the Road Again" by Willie Nelson; "I've Been Everywhere" by Johnny Cash; "Country Roads" by John Denver; "The Long and Winding Road," "Day Tripper," and "Drive My Car" by the Beatles; "Slow Ride" by Foghat; "Little Deuce Coupe" by the Beach Boys; "Get Out of My Dreams (Get into My Car)" by Billy Ocean; "Freeway of Love" by Aretha Franklin; "Truckin'" by the Grateful Dead) other than to say that they reinforce the importance of aimlessness. Unless you are a certified mythic hero with access to the gods, quests tend to be better in prospect than in result.

The general rule seems to be: if you set out from the Promontory of Hope you'll return through the Vale of Melancholy. If you set out to have a beer and a smoke, however, chances are you'll have a nifty adventure and make it home in time for dinner. Paul Fussell notwithstanding, sometimes it's better to be a tourist, not a traveler.

What I was having trouble with was not the Deep South. All my casual experiences in the Heart of Dixie were like life in a slightly foreign country: swamp topography with no brutal winter, the high-minded Ruskin Co-op gone bust, the fatal carelessness of Blakely's peanut-butter plant, the pantomime violence of the Rattlesnake Roundup, the sealed-off quilters of Gee's Bend, the compassion of Willie Campbell, the land-loving squirrel hunter and his dogs in the Free State of Jones, the Baptist oligopoly, the integrated gambling in Natchez, the abstract code of honor invoked on the Vidalia sandbar and throughout the South, the cross-cultural pollination of Ferriday and elsewhere, the visual dreariness and aural excitement, the violence on all sides in Jena, the pugnacious populist Longs in Winnfield, and the never-ending kindness of strangers. I didn't speak the language of Dixie, but I could understand it.

But I was still having trouble understanding the slaughters. I had come to appreciate the importance of land ownership, racial hierarchy, bloodlines, honor, and shame. I could understand how they all fit together and worked like friction plates to spark the killings. But why haven't Colfax and Coushatta been better understood? Why didn't more people know about them? Why didn't we read about them in school? We think that lynching was the worst of it. Not so. Perhaps the lynchings along U.S. 84 are easier to understand than mob killings. Those post-card photos from the 1930s of limp black men hanging from tree limbs like meat slabs at the butcher's are certainly impossible to get out of the mind. Perhaps if the massacres had been photographed. . . .

I started looking at other homegrown slaughters, thinking that if I could find an analogue I'd understand better what happened to my kin in Louisiana. Oddly enough there is one vaguely similar: the so-called Mountain Meadow massacre in southern Utah. In 1857, a wagon train of settlers from Arkansas was moving across the Utah Territory en route to California. The local Mormons, in cahoots with some Indians, wanted the settlers' stuff, especially a large herd of cows. The Mormons were in a siege mentality. They were anxious about being controlled by the U.S. government. They wanted an independent state. So the whites dressed up like Indians and attacked. The emigrants spotted them as frauds, as white Mormons pretending to be Paiutes, and yelled this out. After things quieted down, the Mormons then said that if the settlers would just lay down their guns they would be given safe passage across the territory. The settlers did. Then the Mormons slaughtered them and left their bodies out in the open to rot.

The reason this is like Coushatta is that for the next one hundred years the Mormons were able to stonewall their complicity. They adamantly denied doing the killing. "The Indians did it" sounds a lot like "the Texans did it." In both massacres, the triggering devices seem to be anxiety about land and paranoia about being taken over by outsiders. But the Louisianians were also concerned about the shifting role of blacks as well as their suffocating code of white-only honor. The Mormons trumped this, however. They were doing God's will.

We don't slaughter this way any longer. Massacre has become a government monopoly, whether domestic (Waco, Ruby Ridge) or abroad (My Lai, Fallujah). In the beginning of the twenty-first century, we Americans seem to have replaced group acts of premeditated violence with individual ones. The crazed shooter has replaced the vigilante mob—Fort Hood, Columbine, and Blacksburg. Much of the rest of the world still acts out vengeance with death squads. Maybe parts of Latin America, Africa, and the Far East understand the Deep South better than I ever will. What all these acts of killing have in common is the economy of heroic delusion. Things are being set straight, scales rebalanced, getting back to even.

And that's exactly how the killing in Colfax and Coushatta must have been couched and, if the historical markers and my conversations are proof, still is. Putting *down* a riot is not the same as starting *up* a rampage. Restoring the status quo makes for a more comfortable explanation than mass execution. That's how Jimmy Marston III could have seen the killing of my family as salutary, even redemptive. *Everyone was very happy that Twitchell was gone. We're still happy today that he's gone.* The outsiders had to be put down and out.

As a kid I used to have what I think are the standard dreams of glory. They are daydreams of family protection, and they form the profit center of superhero comics and movies. Things get set straight by young men of steel. Here's the version I locked on to. Ethan Allen led a band of Vermonters during the Revolutionary War. They were a ragtag collection of what today would be called commandos. The English called them terrorists. These Green Mountain Boys stormed Fort Ticonderoga in the dead of night. They took the fort from the tyrannical British. They kicked out the uninvited Redcoats. They made the land safe for the poor farmers and their women.

(It was a shock some years ago to go to Fort Ticonderoga and find out the truth. I'm not sure what the exact truth was, but the fort seems to have been tended by a handful of sleeping soldiers, the Green Mountain Boys climbed up the wall, shushed a sentry, opened up the front door, walked through, and collared the drunk commandant. What they really knew how to do well was to tell a good story.)

What I came to realize is that this is the same restoration story that was being told to youngsters in Louisiana, only that here my kin are the Redcoats, the intruders. Thinking this way, I realized how easily I could have gone over to the Confederate side, how I could have wanted my land back, my culture back, my stained honor back. The postwar South was a world turned upside down, inside out, a decimated world in which not just families had disappeared, but a whole new order had taken its place. Eudora Welty once observed that what is unique to the South is a distinct and superpowerful "sense of place." That's because really that's all they had left.

Good-bye and Stay Warm

So coming home I did not feel like Marlow in *Heart of Darkness*, who had been hollowed out by what he had seen. I didn't get all that I wanted, true, but I didn't get what I feared. Remember how Captain America and Billy, the protagonists in *Easy Rider*, are blasted away by rednecks in a pickup truck in Louisiana? I was concerned enough before I left Florida to find out where they got shot—Morganza, Louisiana, not too far from where the Red River joins the Mississippi.

In fact, I came home thinking how insular and even smug the two regions of MHT's life were: northern New England and the Deep South. Had the North lost the war and Vermont been occupied by southern carpetbaggers, how different would matters have been? Would I now be proudly proclaiming how we Yankees showed the overreaching Rebels the door? Yes, probably. I don't think we would have had those massacres, however. We deal with a different kind of honor and shame. Ours is mixed in with money and greed. Violence comes in many hues; only some of them blood red.

At the end of one of Robert Frost's poems ("Good-bye and Keep Cold"), the poet is turning to leave Vermont and he says to his apple orchard that he hopes it stays really cold during the winter. To grow and flourish it needs colder weather than he can endure. Why it needs such brutal cold is not to be understood. "Something," Frost writes, "has to be left to God." Maybe that's what Faulkner is saying about the South: "To understand the world, you must first understand a place like Mississippi," knowing full well that even he can't understand this state. Places, like people, have lives of their own. They grow and change at their own pace. They have their own histories, their own unique coordinates, their own reality and delusions.

So maybe that's how best for me to say good-bye to Deep Dixieland. In so many ways it's still terra incognita. Instead of trying to unite regions, maybe there's something to be said for rejoicing in their differences. Or in some of their differences. Perhaps some things cannot and should not be fully understood, are best left to God. Maybe X and Y axes should cross only occasionally. Maybe some things are better not known. As Oscar Wilde said, "The brotherhood of man is not a mere poet's dream: it is a most depressing and humiliating reality." I'm already forgetting the assassin's name. I can picture his gravestone, but I'd never be able to find the graveyard. I'm not asking. It's deep in the woods. I'll tell them that. My grandchildren won't know his name, nor should they. Time to break camp, furl the flags, make peace, move on.

Acknowledgments

L loved this project. It came at a difficult time in my life, and it gave me something to concentrate on that was both introspective and out in the world. Plus, doing it moved me from the computer screen back to the yellow pads. To write it, I had to get off my butt and move around.

Trying to understand my kinsman was inspiring. If ever there was someone who should have curled up and rolled over, here he was. At thirty-five, his life was an ungodly mess. And yet he not just persevered through terrible trauma, he created a whole new life for himself. Yes, he made mistakes—a few whoppers—but he never shirked, never shied away, never said uncle. Well, okay, maybe this was because he was never really introspective: I don't know. He spent his formative years on the battlefield taking orders from commanders, not on the couch listening to Mr. Rogers. Self-contemplation was not MHT's strong suit. But I do know that he was right about big subjects. He knew what Dixie was, sooner or later, going to have to do. Not to sound too spooky, but from time to time on my trip across U.S. 84, I could almost see him up ahead beckoning me, encouraging me, assuring me to come on and take a look.

Along with getting to know my kinsman, I enjoyed coming to know the South. Although I live here, I really haven't paid much attention to it. So having to see Dixie up close in order to understand what happened to my great-grandfather was an adventure in doing something I have trouble with: paying attention to detail. I had to go slow. I had to just sit and stew. Usually when I have to go somewhere I try to figure out the quickest route and then follow it, but here I was taking the slowest route and even then getting lost.

I met wonderful people along the way. Starting off in Waycross, Georgia, I was helped by a retired reporter for the *Waycross Journal-Herald* (Larry Purdom) and a reference librarian (James Britton) in the Waycross–Ware County Public Library. They showed me all the stuff they had on the Ruskin Co-op, even giving me stacks of raw and refined material. Next we had a delightful time with John Lewis, a shopkeeper at the Bargain Depot in Homerville, who took the afternoon to explain all the hard goods that someone in the nineteenth century would have needed to eke a living from this beaten-up land. In Valdosta, we got quite a dose of new-style Baptist religion at CrossPointe Church, and at the Rattlesnake Roundup in Whigham we got a taste of the old-style religion of handling the serpent.

I want to thank Jon and Louise Fairbank, dear friends from Vermont, for getting into the rattlin' spirit of snakiness. They also got us into RV-ing as they had taken a trip across the South in a VW Rialta, a peewee version of the Winnebago View. They clued us in on the joys of purposeful wandering.

Before saying good-bye to Georgia, I must also thank John Edmondson, an avuncular museum helper at the Early County Museum, and especially George Gray of Early Company Gin Inc. George would bring the entire two-story gin machine to a throbbing halt so he could stick his hand into the knife thrasher and pull out seeds to show us. His afternoon of kindness to strangers, Yankee strangers at that, merits more than a tip of the hat. His sentence, "Y'all are rude and we are all ignorant," captured for me the essence of regional prejudice. It's true, yes, just not true enough.

Our biggest help in Alabama was my old graduate school chum Bob Cohan. Bob always wanted to be a rabbi, and so he was a great source of information on how the Jews made their way into the South, how they got past the barriers that kept other foreigners out, and how they made their peace with people who didn't always hold them in high regard. And vice versa. Plus, Bob loves to take afternoon naps with his two golden labs, so after a burst of rabbinical studies we would both fall sound asleep surrounded by the snoring pups. Bob also got me off the hook with the Gee's Bend women by buying a little quilt. He knows what a tightwad I am.

The day Bob left to go back to Florida was the day we met Willie Campbell. Willie impressed me from the get-go. When I told him what I was interested in, he understood at once and filled me in with stories of what it was like to be in a world where skin color pretty much trumped all other conditions. His melancholy resignation wasn't maudlin or self-pitying; it was stoic and even redemptive. As I say earlier, nothing is so unsettling to a skeptic as an honest-to-God Christian.

In Mississippi almost everyone was friendly. The salespeople at Walmart, the docents at the Lauren Rogers Museum, the parishioners at the Salem Heights Baptist Church, the rangers at the Lincoln State Park, and especially all those helpers at the Isle of Capri in Natchez, who just wanted to relieve us of our excess cash. But the real stand-out was Jeffrey Woods, the squirrel hunter and breeder of those long-legged pooches. If we had let him, I'm sure we could have spent the night, eaten his squirrel gumbo, and been serenaded to sleep by the yelping feists. From the questions we asked him, he must have thought we were the stupidest Yankees in the world. If so, he and Darlene politely kept it to themselves.

What can I say about Louisiana, the place where my family almost came undone? Where can you go in this entire country and meet up with Jerry Lee Lewis's sister and have her show you around the family house without so much as a "come back later, I'm busy"? Where can you drive around a town like Jena with Carl Smith, the retired sheriff, and have him be willing to share his personal views with a total outsider, an outsider who he must suspect is critical of his culture? We get to Winnfield, and the Louisiana Political Museum and Hall of Fame is closed. Carolyn Phillips, director as well as a commissioner of El Camino East/West Corridor, opens it up just for us and regales us with stories of both state politics and highway politics. They are often connected. And how about Ben Littlepage, the pecan magnate and owner of the infamous Colfax cannon, who, although he was on the West Coast at the time, calls up Sam Daniels, his plantation foreman, and tells him to give us run of the place? Not only did we see every aspect of pecan production as well as the Calhoun slave cabins, but we ended up with bags of shelled nuts that we were eating for weeks.

We also spent a few days with Jeff and Judy Schneider in southern Louisiana. The Schneiders were Yankees who came into the South after the war. They came to harvest and mill the swamp timber. The family so completely adapted that Jeff has a small outbuilding that looks like a Cabela's outpost filled with all his hunting and fishing gear. As far as I could see, it was the only building on his estate that was locked. Not only did Jeff and Judy share their insights into southern culture, they also treated us like visiting dignitaries, not the itinerant freeloaders we were.

You can't tell me southern hospitality is just a social construct, a façade, a made-up bit of passive aggression. I can assure you that you won't find this generosity in New England. People in Deep Dixie are openhearted in a way I've never known. They are hospitable and not just to perfect strangers but to not-so-perfect strangers. Okay, maybe the same thing can be said about smiling cannibals seasoning you to taste in the boiling pot, but no matter: I appreciated it.

And what of Avery Hamilton, who spent most of a day showing eight of us chattering busybodies around Colfax, indulging our ignorance and giving us a history lesson that was not just fair-minded but compassionate to all sides. Again I was seeing from a black man that much-touted side of Christianity that seems a bit missing from the world to which I am more accustomed.

And that brings me to the two men who more than any others really treated us like royalty, albeit royalty from an ancient and not entirely forgotten antagonist. I must say, I was anxious about meeting Jimmy Marston. After all, if blood is important, then what we should have between us is bad blood. I had seen the PBS show on Reconstruction a number of times, and so I expected a stars and bars–waving bullyboy. But nothing of the kind. He was gracious to a tee and understood how confused we were about what had happened years ago, maybe even sympathetic with us because perhaps at some level he was confused too. How much do we ever know, truly know, about received truth? Are there any stories more suspect than stories that are cast as not being stories at all? Families, of course, are built on such unexamined figments. Wars get fought over them. That he was willing to share with us all the vestiges of his family tradition—the diary, the glasses, the deeds, the pictures—is something we won't soon forget.

Nor will we ever forget Mildred Worrell, his aide-de-camp and keeper of the Marston homestead in Clinton, Louisiana. When I told her that I was planning on following U.S. 84 across the South, she said in a deep drawl, "Honey, you don't need to take that road, just get yourselves over here and we'll explain it all to ya'll." I don't doubt she was right.

And best for last: Joe Taylor. Joe has helped my family explore their roots before. Bits and pieces of the family call him when they are coming to Coushatta, and he takes time to show them around. You can't do it without him because so much of the history is now underwater. When I wrote him and told him that another wave of Twitchells was about to flow through, he didn't gallop off to Texas but dedicated four days to showing us around. He was the consummate tour guide: he would explain what he knew and how he knew it, take us to the place it happened, and then step back and let us come to grips with it. He and his gracious wife, Susan, had a dinner party for us and those Coushattans who were also interested in these stories. It was impossible not to come away thinking, hey, I'm not so sure of what I'm sure of.

Everyone else I'm indebted to knows who they are, especially Mary.

And now, since you've been willing to wade through this tide of gratitude, I'll tell you a little secret. You know all those articles and news reports about where to live the good life, how to make do on just pennies a day, how to retire at fifty and live like a king? Well, I'll tell you how to do it. Get a cheap RV and spend time in the state park campgrounds of the Deep South states. Not only are they a great bargain (cheaper if you're a senior, cheaper still if you join the states' discount clubs, and almost free if you stay in parks developed by the Corps of Engineers), they are also in the most interesting spots, near a woodsy park or on the side of a pleasant lake. They never seemed to be full and were always neat. I must say that part of me thinks it's unfair that RV owners get such special treatment, but the rest of me says it's okay. Anyone who feels at home in a sardine can ought to get a break.